Keeping My Confidence

Even Though I Feel Conflicted

by

DANIEL VOSS

ISBN: 978-0-578-41229-0

DEDICATION

I dedicate this book to my bride, Amy Lynn,

and the bride of Christ, the local church.

I have given my life to you both.

It was the best decision I ever made.

CONTENTS

INTRODUCTION

I want to do what is right, but I can't. I want to do what is good, but I don't. I don't want to do what is wrong, but I do it anyway. Oh, what a miserable person I am! - The Apostle Paul

I have a confession. I am a pastor and I have a problem. I have confidence in who God is, but I am conflicted in how He works. I know, I know, pastors are not supposed to think like this, but I do. Maybe that's the problem; I'm not like most pastors. I'm more raw than religious. More passionate than polished. More authentic than prophetic. Sometimes I am even more vulnerable than virtuous. I don't have a horrendous past I have been redeemed from. I wasn't given a platform. I don't have a pastoral pedigree. In fact, most of my family doesn't even attend church. As a result, I am more comfortable in a room full of sinners than a room full of saints. To be honest, the only time I feel out of place is in a room full of pastors. That's a problem. It's not the only problem I have; I have many.

I have faith but sometimes I have doubt. I believe in prayer but don't pray as much as I should. I believe God is able but sometimes doubt He is willing. I believe the best but often prepare for the worst. I know I am a masterpiece but feel like a mess. I have anticipation about tomorrow but am overwhelmed with anxiety today. I am grateful but act greedy. I am content but constantly strive for more. I am cooperative but extremely competitive. I am more than a conqueror but often feel less than capable. Should I go on? I try to keep life simple but have way too much going on. I am surrounded by others but feel all alone. I love Jesus but people annoy me. I love my wife and kids more than anything but I am easily agitated by them. I ask for God to use me but often complain about being used.

I am conflicted.

Every belief, every blessing, every promise, every prayer has a "but" attached to it. I believe…but. I know…but. I am…but. I will try…but.

No matter how hard I try I cannot kick the "buts."

Pardon My But

Isn't it funny how one little three letter word, can make all the difference in the world? The word "but" is full of unlimited possibilities and endless pain. I love you, but. The results were good, but. He's a great kid, but. You're a wonderful employee, but.

It doesn't matter who you are, where you're from, or what you have done, the word "but" has power. It creates tension and adds suspense. We received your application, but. We saw your audition, but.

What's on the other side of "but?" Good news or bad news? Did he get the job or not? Did she get the role or was she rejected? Someone please tell me.

Honey, I'm pregnant, but. Is it my kid? Is the baby healthy? Is there more than one? OMG. The "but" is bugging me!

Not only does it add suspense, but it also causes heartache. You're a good wife, but. You're pretty, but. I had fun, but. That was great, but. Thank you, but.

How many needless fights and continuous arguments has the word "but" started?

According to the dictionary the word "but" is a conjunction. By its very definition a conjunction is the action or instance of two or more events occurring at the same point in time or in the same space.

I'm not sure about you, but that describes me all the time. I have two or more actions or events or thoughts or feelings playing out in the same space at the same time, all the time.

So by its very nature, the word "but" is conflicting.

If James, the little brother of Jesus, is right when he says, "a double minded man is unstable in all his ways," it's no wonder I feel so crazy and have a headache all the time. I am conflicted. The "but" is too big and occupying way too much space.

Same Problem Different Person

I don't think you are much different than me. You love your spouse, but sometimes you wonder if they are the devil in disguise. You love your kids, but sometimes you question if you are entertaining demons unaware. You believe in healing, but you're still sick. You know God can provide, but you're still broke. You know God gives peace, but you still can't sleep at night. For goodness sake, you love God, but sometimes it seems He is taking a nap and has forgotten you. That leads to more conflict. I love God, but it doesn't seem as if He loves me.

I've been around church people long enough to know some of you would never admit you have had these thoughts. At least not publicly. Let me indulge you for a moment. Let's say you have all your doubts settled, your fears removed, and your worries relieved. Maybe you are steadfast and immovable, always abounding in the work of the Lord with a smile on your face and a song in your heart. Well then, this book isn't for you. Instead, I beg you to write your own book and please tell us how you do it. I would love to know how you sleep so soundly when the storm is raging, the wind is howling, the waves are crashing, and the boat starts rocking. I want to know how you raise your kids in a world full of evil without developing ulcers. Please tell us how you stay so calm when the stock market drops, when the account runs low, and the boss says we are downsizing. Teach us how you never lose your confidence in such a conflicting world.

I know you love Jesus. So do I! I know you pray. So do I! I know you read the Bible. For crying out loud, I read it for a living! I know you attend church. I am a pastor; I live at the church! How in the world are you so calm, collected, and confident when the rest of us feel so crazy?

Maybe I'm wrong. Maybe this book is just for me and writing is my form of therapy.

Maybe it's my parents' fault. That sounds about right. Nature and nurture created this turmoil. But the problem with that theory is my parents were actually pretty cool. They weren't perfect, but they did the best they could.

Maybe it was my life experiences. Something happened in my childhood or adolescence that caused this chaos. Yes, that's it. Well not really, because my childhood was great.

Maybe it was a bad relationship that developed this discord within me. No, that can't be it either. My wife and I were high school sweethearts and she is still the apple of my eye.

Maybe it was a bad decision and karma is just paying me back. I don't think that's it either. I have felt this way as long as I can remember.

Whose fault is it then? The Devil? Adam? Eve? The Media? Facebook?

Does it really matter?

Not really.

God never puts our destiny in someone else's hands.

Not the Only One

After twenty years of ministry I know there are others just like me. In fact, I believe I'm in good company. Some of the greatest pastors and theologians of all time dealt with bouts of inner conflict. Some of the greatest men and women in the Bible were conflicted.

Abraham, the friend of God, was conflicted.

Moses, a man who knew God face to face, was conflicted.

David, a man after God's own heart, was conflicted.

Even Mary, the mother of Jesus, was conflicted.

John the Baptist, the forerunner of Jesus. The man whom Jesus described as being the greatest man ever born to a woman, was conflicted.

Then there's Peter, the Rock. He was certainly conflicted.

And Paul, the author of almost half the New Testament.

Let me go one step further.

Would you believe me if I said Jesus, God in the flesh, the Messiah, the Alpha and Omega, the Word Incarnate, was conflicted?

Troubles and trials know no prejudice. Suffering and sickness are a universal experience. Conflict is a part of life. So maybe it's not conflict that is our problem; maybe it is our response to it. As we all know, two people can face the very same circumstance with very different outcomes. What causes one person to become bitter causes the other person to get better. What is a stumbling block to one is a stepping stone to another.

Why? Perspective.

Randy Alcorn said, "Nothing is more important to suffering (conflict) than the perspective we bring to it."

The longer I am in ministry and the more I deal with people, the more I understand life really is all about perspective. It's not so much what happens to you, but how you perceive what happens to you that matters.

My prayer is this book will give you a different perspective.

I don't know if the conflict ever really goes away. I am not even convinced it needs to go away.

As weird as it may sound, I believe you can find confidence in conflict. I think God does His best work in conflict. No one wants to admit it, but it is through conflict that our character is developed and our faith grows. Character gives us hope even when we're walking through hell. All you need is the right perspective.

So whatever conflict you are in, you can be confident knowing God is with you. You will make it to the other side. You just need a higher perspective to see it.

That is what I hope this book provides.

By providing biblical examples of those who have gone before us, I hope to give you a better sense of perspective. I still believe anything God did at any other time, He can do now. Anything He did at any other place, He can do here. Anything He did through any person, He can do through you.

You just need to believe it, so let your struggles strengthen your faith.

Before we get started on this journey together I want to personally say thank you for taking the time to read this book. It is my highest honor that you would allow me to speak into your life, and I promise you, I have not taken this opportunity lightly.

I believe this book will help your confidence in God grow, even though you may be conflicted in how He works.

Are you ready to have some fun?

Let's get started.

THE CHAPTER BEFORE CHAPTER 1
PUT PERSPECTIVE IN ITS PROPER PLACE

I grew up in a small town just outside Tulsa, Oklahoma. I graduated with eighty-six kids. Half of them were cousins. We had one stoplight, one bank, no Post Office, and two convenient stores. It was a real bidding war for business.

In small town middle America, high school football is king. The name "Coach" is the most revered name in the land. Football is what we talk about around the dinner table, at the corner store, in the church lobby, and at the one stoplight. Football is a religion for six months out of the year.

At my house, we talked about football, deer season, work and church. In that order. The town I grew up in had a population of 2,500 people. We would have over 4,000 thousand people attend our football games. If it was an away game; well, you could have robbed every house in town. Andy and Barney were escorting the football team.

As you can imagine, I love football.

However, there was one event that took place every Friday night that never made sense to me. Promise not to get mad? Promise to save your hate mail? Promise? Cross your heart, hope to die, stick 10,000 needles in your eye? I know I'm treading on thin ice, but here it goes. The one event that took place every Friday night that made absolutely no sense to me was the half-time show put on by the marching band.

This isn't a jock vs. the band thing. Our band was actually very good. For the longest time they won the only state championship our school had ever experienced. If my memory serves me correctly, they won thirteen years in a row.

However, from my perspective, whether that be standing on the sideline or outside the locker room, it never made sense. Sure, I could hear the music and it sounded nice, but the uniforms, the instruments, the people who threw weird things up in the air and the constant movement looked like pure chaos.

I will never forget the day my perspective changed.

Is This Heaven?

After graduating high school, my older brother got a job where he could afford season tickets to the Holy Grail of football in the state of Oklahoma, the University of Oklahoma Sooners. Because he is such a good brother he invited me to one of their games. I still remember walking into the stadium for the first time. I was amazed at its sheer size. The sights. The smells. The sounds. They were glorious!

Was this heaven? No, it was just the Gaylord Family Memorial Stadium. Home of the seven time National Champion Sooners. Boomer Sooner baby!

Gig 'Em

The visiting team that day was the University of Texas A & M Aggies. The first half went back and forth. It was fast paced, heart pounding, and I was having the time of my life. It was thirty minutes of football in its purest form. No one sat down, no one went to the restrooms, and no one dared go to the concession stand.

As the first half ended and halftime approached, 90,000 other people and I decided to take a break at the same time. My older, much wiser brother, stopped me and said, "Daniel, you don't want to miss halftime."

I said, "Are you serious, Clark? Why would I stay for halftime?"

He said, "You don't want to miss the band."

I replied, "Are you my brother? Did you just tell me to stay for the band?"

He said, "Sit down. This one is worth watching."

Not wanting to offend the guy who brought me to my first real football game, I figured I better do what he said.

What I saw next changed my perspective forever. The drum major took his place on the stand. He blew the whistle and three hundred plus cadets dressed in military uniforms took the field. For the next few minutes I was mesmerized. I had never seen anything like this. They performed with precision and perfection. Constant movement formed multiple geometric signs and shapes. I was stunned. What I thought was chaotic before was actually creating the most beautiful images. It was unlike anything I had ever seen.

I fell in love with the marching band.

What changed? My perspective.

A different perspective changed the way I viewed the band. A higher perspective allowed me to rise above what I thought looked like a mess and see the masterpiece in motion.

Get High and Keep Walking

Gaylord Family Memorial Stadium is huge. It is the twenty-third largest stadium in the world and from where I was sitting I never felt closer to God. Literally, I was that high up.

Getting higher allowed me to see things differently. After watching the Texas A&M marching band I made the decision to never judge things from a ground level perspective again.

From that moment on, I knew I would need to get higher to see things more clearly.

Too many people miss out on golden opportunities because they are limited by their ground level perspective.

In the middle of your current situation you may only see confusion and chaos. Chaos leads to conflict so you need to rise above your situation. The only way to rise above your current situation is by faith. Faith allows you to see things from a higher perspective. Just like sitting forty rows higher at a football stadium, a higher perspective allows you to see how all things are coming together.

Let me give you a biblical example.

One of the most comforting passages in the Bible is Psalm 23. Right smack in the middle of the Psalm is verse four. David says, "Yea, (Notice it doesn't say yippee or yasss!) though I walk through the valley of the shadow of death, I will fear no evil: for thou art with me; thy rod and thy staff they comfort me." KJV

As you know, life is full of peaks and valleys. To some degree every one of us will find ourselves in one valley or another. Whether it be a sickness or loss of a job or marriage. It could even be the loss of your hopes and dreams. Maybe your children have walked away. Maybe they weren't born as healthy as you would have liked. Maybe your dream job is a living nightmare. Maybe it is the valley of depression or anxiety or fear. Maybe it's a valley known as: a thyroid, heart disease, cancer, back pain, knee problems or a financial deficit. Whatever your valley is, I want to acknowledge it is real.

But it's a valley.

What makes a valley a valley? A valley has a beginning and an end. An entry and an exit point is what separates a valley from a grave. However, from your vantage point you may not know it's a valley. It may feel more like a grave.

David knew all about valleys. It was his job as a shepherd to lead his sheep through them and his job as a king to lead his nation through them.

Between Bethlehem and Jerusalem there were many wilderness areas containing valleys. Sheep had to be moved from pasture to pasture, so he had no choice but to go through them. The valleys were very dangerous. With the changing of the seasons, increase of rain, wild animals and nomadic thieves, you never knew what was lurking around each bend.

In 1 Samuel 17 David told Saul he had to kill lions and bears to protect his flock. Hiding in every shadow was a chance of death. No doubt he lost some sheep along the way. Even after he was anointed king he still had to go through some very real valleys. King Saul and his army searched every mountain top and valley low to kill David. So when he said, "I walk through the valley of the shadow of death," he wasn't kidding. He is acknowledging valleys are a very real part of life. He wishes they weren't, but they are. He wishes he could have avoided them, but he couldn't.

But, and this is a big "but," just because he had to walk through them, doesn't mean he had to stay in them.

He said, "I walk through the valley."

The word "through" makes all the difference in the world.

In other words, David said, "Even though I walk in the valley of the shadow of death, it does not mean I will stay in the valley of the shadow of death. I am making up my mind right here, right now, that I will walk through it. I will come out the other side. I am not bringing my Coleman sleeping bag or gas lantern. I'm not bringing a change of clothes or my Rambo lunch pail because I don't plan on staying here. Even though I might have to walk through it, I don't plan on staying in it. I may have to visit the valley, but I will not take a vacation there."

No Camping Allowed

I don't know what you are going through right now, but please let me encourage you to keep walking. Don't settle in your valley. Don't get too comfortable. This is not the place to stop and rest. Now is not the time to lie down and take a nap. I will lie down in green pastures and rest beside the still waters, but I will keep walking through the valley. I may be in it, but I will pass through it.

There is hope on the other side. No matter what you are going through today, if there was an entry point, then there is an exit point. It might not end quickly. It might be days, it might be weeks, it might even be years, but every valley has an end. So please don't grow weary in the midst of your valley. This too will pass. It might pass like a kidney stone, but it will pass.

David knows this. This is why he wrote, "Weeping may stay for the night, but rejoicing comes in the morning." (Psalm 30:5) NIV

It may be night, but morning is coming. The sun will shine again. And when it does, you will see the Good Shepherd led you through a barren place to get you to a better place.

How do I know? I have read the rest of the Psalm. May I remind you verse four is in the middle.

Some of you may feel stuck in the middle too. You are not where you want to be just yet, but you have a choice. You can throw a tantrum, you can kick and scream, you can lie down and complain. No one will blame you if you do. You have every right. However, I need you to know, if you want to make it through the valley faster, you need to keep walking. Pouting won't help. Whining won't help. Shaking your fist at God won't help. Blogging won't help. Facebooking won't help.

Every minute you spend complaining about your situation is another minute you waste not walking through your valley.

If you don't have the strength to walk, crawl.

If you can't crawl, roll.

If you can't roll, scrape your way through the valley.

Just keep moving forward.

Don't settle in the valley.

Don't park in the pit.

No storm, no sickness, no pain, no valley is ever permanent.

If all you can do is let it rain, then hold on and hang in there, because the sun will appear again. Every storm eventually runs out of rain. I promise.

If it hasn't worked out yet, then it's not over yet.

Your destiny is not a mystery, it is a decision to keep moving forward. To get out of your hell you need hope to see what others can't see. You need to keep believing God has something better in store for you than sitting in a valley being a victim. Keep your head up and keep walking. Keep walking when the clouds of doubt roll in. Keep walking when no one believes in you. Keep walking when confusion sets in. Keep walking because He who began a good work in you will carry it through until the day of completion. Tell yourself, "I will find pleasure in this valley. I will find purpose in this valley. I will find something to praise God for in this valley." Life may take some strange twists and turns, but the One who holds the future is still in control. God has you in this place for a reason. The lessons learned in the valley prepare us for what's ahead. God does His best work in the valley because He always chooses to do a work in our heart before we can do a work for Him. Our character has to match our calling, and unfortunately, character is developed through conflict. So keep walking and hold on to hope. Whatever you do, don't fall victim to the valley.

No One Wants to Camp Alone

I know it may feel like you are all alone, but notice what David says next, "I will fear no evil for thou art with me."

No matter how bad, how barren or how bleak it is, God is always before, beside and behind you. He gave us the promise He will never leave us.

You are never walking alone.

Up until this point David has been using third person. He's been telling us how awesome his Shepherd is. Now that he is in a valley he shifts to second person singular. In other words, he stopped telling us about the Shepherd and starts talking to the Shepherd.

He says, "You are with me. Your rod and staff comfort me."

His poem has become a prayer.

When worry comes, you have two choices: You can pray or you can panic. If you prayed as much as you panicked, you'd have a whole lot less to worry about.

Don't worry about anything; instead, pray about everything. Tell God what you need, and thank him for all He has done. Then you will experience God's peace, which exceeds anything we can understand. His peace will guard your hearts and minds as you live in Christ Jesus. (Philippians 4:6-7) NLT

The valley is still there. It hasn't gone away. I can see it, but I won't fall victim to it because I know who I have walking with me.

So instead of parking in the valley, I am going to start praising God in the valley because God has given me the Good Shepherd, and the Good Shepherd has given me peace.

I know, I know, you tried that.

Can I be honest? I don't think you really did. I think you worried about it, talked about it, whined about it, complained about it, vlogged about it, tweeted about it, called your mom and asked what you should do about it. Then called it prayer. You told every other person about it and when they couldn't help you, you decided God couldn't help you. That's not prayer. That's worry. Prayer is a transfer of trust. From me to Him. How do I know I have stopped worrying about it? I stop talking about it!

There comes a point when you need to stop talking to people about the problem and start talking to the Shepherd about the problem. I even double dog dare you to stop reminding God of your problem and start reminding Him of His promises. Isaiah encouraged the Israelites to put God in remembrance of His promises and to give Him no rest until they come to pass. (Isaiah 62:7)

My kids have a hard time remembering their homework and chores but one thing they are good at remembering is my promises. They will remind me over and over again what I said until I fulfill my end of the bargain. As their dad I will do everything within my power to bring that promise to pass.

God wants to do the same for you. God will not go against His promises.

Paul says no matter how many promises God has made, they are "Yes" in Christ. (2 Corinthians 1:20) NIV

If you feel all alone, remind God of the promises He made toward you. God, You said You will never leave me. God, You said Your rod and staff will comfort me. God, You said Your peace will guard me. God, not a word You say will fall to the ground without coming to pass. From this moment on, I am not going to consider my circumstances any longer, I am going to consider You. I am shifting the focus from my problems to Your promises.

I Will Not…

David goes on to say, "Because I know God is with me, I will fear no evil." The grammar suggests he is using future tense. He seems to be talking about a problem he hasn't even experienced yet.

In other words, he says, "I will not pay for tomorrow's problems with today's peace." Joyce Meyer says, "Worry is a down payment on a problem you may never have."

But even if all of your greatest fears happen, God still promises to give you the strength to get through what you go through.

David knew he would never make it through on his own. So he asked God to give him a higher perspective. He prayed, "From the ends of the earth I call to you, I call as my heart grows faint; lead me to the rock that is higher than I. For You have been a refuge for me, a tower of strength against the enemy." (Psalm 61:2-3) NIV

A tower stands above the battlefield providing a different perspective. It allows us to see the enemy approaching. It also allows us to see more clearly the weapons we have at our disposal.

Perhaps this is why David said, "I will fear no evil: for thou art with me; thy rod and thy staff they comfort me." (Psalm 23:4) KJV

From a higher perspective David can see that the Shepherd is with him, and in His hand, is a rod.

David is familiar with the rod. He used a similar one to kill the lion and bear. He also knows a rod symbolizes power and authority.

From a higher vantage point David now sees he has the power and authority over this valley. The valley has lost its sting. Now it's just a shadow. Sure, it's still scary, but would you rather be hit by a bus or the shadow of the bus?

Daddy Please Help

My children are at the age where they don't think they need me anymore…until they run up against something they can't handle on their own. I'm always there, but they don't get my help nor want my help until a crisis arises. The crisis causes a renewed awareness of their need for me.

When they cry out for help, not only do they receive my presence, but they also receive my power.

David knows this. Therefore, his conflict is what helps develop his confidence.

Thou preparest a table before me in the presence of mine enemies: thou anointest my head with oil; my cup runneth over. Surely goodness and mercy shall follow me all the days of my life: and I will dwell in the house of the LORD forever. (Psalm 23:5-6) KJV

No matter what conflict he is in. No matter who it is against. No matter how bad, barren, or bleak the situation may appear. David knew God is with him. Not only did he know God was with him, he also knew God would bless him. Even in the middle of the valley, he could be blessed.

I need you to know it is possible to be blessed in the middle of your problems. God can bless you in the middle of your pain. He can bless you in the middle of your divorce. Crazy as it sounds He can even bless you in the middle of your sickness or in the middle of your heartache. So don't let your pain, your prison, your problems, or your valley, keep you from your blessing.

It's too easy to feel all alone, but you are not.

Moses told the Israelites, "Be strong and courageous. Do not be afraid or terrified because of them, for the Lord your God goes with you; he will never leave you nor forsake you." (Deuteronomy 31:6) NIV

He will be with you through your loss. He will be with you through your sickness. He will be with you through your divorce. He will be with you when you feel insignificant. He will be with you when you feel like you can't go on.

Not only will He be with you, but He will also give you the power to get through it. I promise, you will get what you need to get through what you go through.

Every. Single. Time.

This reason alone is enough reason to be confident.

Sermon in a sentence: If God brought me to it, He'll get me through it.

FAVORED BUT FRUSTRATED

CH

APTER 1

THE STORY OF MARY

Who runs the world? Girls.

Thank you Beyoncé for that epiphany. However, I disagree. Girls don't run the world. Please forgive me Queen B for saying, but I think William Wallace was more accurate when he stated, "The hand that rocks the cradle rules the world." I think we need to be more specific: moms run the world. Don't be too sad Miss Fierce, I do agree that women are smart enough to make "these" millions and strong enough to bare those children.

Here's to all the ladies out there!

Mother's Day Dilemma

Due to the enormous amount of respect I have for mothers, writing a sermon for Mother's Day is always a struggle. What can I possibly say that would be eloquent enough to articulate the true value of a mother? Few things are as powerful as the tears and tender touch that a mother provides.

One Mother's Day two young children presented their mother with a small plant. The older of the two said with a sad face, "Mommy, we are sorry but this was the best we could do. There was another bouquet we really wanted to buy from the flower shop but it was too expensive. It was really nice and it had a really pretty ribbon on it." "What did the ribbon say?" mom asked. "Rest in Peace," the boy replied. "We thought you would love it since you're always asking for a little peace so you can rest."

On Mother's Day, children will do their absolute best to find something special for their mother. Some will even go to great lengths to make a personal card to express their true feelings.

For instance:

Angie, age eight, wrote: "Dear Mother, I'm going to make dinner for you on Mother's Day. It's going to be a surprise. P.S. I hope you like pizza and popcorn."

Robert said: "I got you a turtle for Mother's Day. I hope you like the turtle better than the snake I got you last year."

Diane wrote: "I hope you like the flowers I got you for Mother's Day. I picked them myself when Mr. Smith wasn't looking."

Who can forget Carol's card: "Dear Mother, I got you what you are always searching for: Two aspirin. Happy Mother's Day!"

While these letters aren't exactly perfect, these children did their absolute best to show their mother how much they love her.

It is because of our great love for mothers that many countries throughout the world have honored them with a special day since the 1600's. In America, Mother's Day became an official holiday by presidential decree in 1914.

The desire to honor our mothers is not a new concept. In Exodus 20 God declared all of His children were to honor their father and mother. In fact, the fifth commandment is the first commandment with a promise attached to it.

Honor your father and mother. Then you will live a long, full life in the land the LORD your God is giving you. (Exodus 20:12) NLT

It appears mothers have always had a special place in God's heart. This may surprise you, but the term "helpmate" given to Eve is also the same Hebrew word used to describe God many times in Scripture.

He even compares the love He has for His children to a mother's love.

I will comfort you there in Jerusalem as a mother comforts her child. (Isaiah 66:13) NLT

Jesus said, "How often I have wanted to gather your children together as a hen protects her chicks beneath her wings, but you wouldn't let me." (Luke 13:34) NLT

Man wasn't complete, the family wasn't complete, and creation wasn't complete until God made mothers. The term mother is indicative of one who is more than a parent. Biology is the least of what makes someone a good mother.

The biblical word translated for mother is the Hebrew word "AM-Eh." It means the bond of the family. This word signifies a force that strengthens and holds all things together. I certainly am not diminishing the role of father in the family, but I think we would all agree that mom is the glue that holds the family together.

Millions of Americans credit their mother as the main influence upon their lives. Abraham Lincoln said, "All that I am, or hope to be, I owe to my angel mother."

I would say the same thing about my mother.

Love you mom. (Sorry dad.)

Someone once pointed out that of the sixty-nine kings of France, only three were truly loved by their subjects. Those three were the only ones raised by their own mothers.

Mother Mary?

Let me pose a hypothetical question: If you had to choose someone else to raise your child, who would you choose and why? If you were looking for the perfect mother to leave your child with, who would she be? Would she be wealthy? Would looks be important? How about an education? Would she have other children? Is fame important? How about genetics? Seriously, if you could put pen to paper and describe the perfect mother to raise your children, what would she be like?

How about Martha Stewart?

What about Oprah?

Mrs. June Cleaver?

Mrs. Carol Brady?

Peggy Bundy?

Judge Judy?

The Pioneer Woman?

I know who you would pick… Joanna Gaines.

For God, this question wasn't hypothetical. When He determined to send Jesus to save the world, He had to choose a mother—a mother who would be responsible for the raising of His only Son.

Talk about stress!

Mary was hand-picked by the God of the universe to bring the Savior of the universe into the world. She was personally responsible to nurture and care for Him until the day of His death on the cross.

There must have been something about Mary.

What was it? The Bible really doesn't say.

We know she was a small-town girl from the insignificant village of Nazareth. Though she was of nobility, being in the line of King David, the family had lost all its status because of the years of Israel's captivity and foreign domination. Mary was raised as a humble peasant girl, not an honorable princess.

Super Mary?

Nowhere in the Bible is Mary given supernatural abilities. Parenting was the same for Mary as it probably is for you or your parents.

If there is one word that describes parenting for almost everyone it is the word conflicted. Wouldn't you agree? Seriously, for a brief moment, please take off your supermom or dad cape and admit parenting is often chaotic. If you don't have children yet, enjoy the peace and tranquility now; your time is coming. Don't believe everything you see on social media. The same woman who just posted, "these kids are my breath," is the same woman who was just out of breath for screaming at those kids. That's the problem with Pinterest. They only show you what they want you to see…through a filter.

Can we at least agree parenting is confusing? My goodness, raising anything is chaotic and confusing. Ever had a puppy? No matter how much money you spend training them, they will use the bathroom wherever they want, whenever they want. And if you have cat, I'm sorry. Those things are creepy and weird. They use the bathroom inside, hack up hair balls constantly, and stare at you while you sleep. Plus, let's get real. You don't own a cat. A cat does what it wants, when it wants.

Sorry for offending all the cat lovers…but it's true.

Back to the topic.

Parenting doesn't always make sense. It is conflicting. I know you love your child but come on, sometimes they act like terrorists. There will never be anything you love as much, but annoys you as much, as your children.

What I have learned over the past thirty-nine years of life is that so much of life is about staying power. Parenting is the surest test of willpower there is.

My mother raised three boys, plus my dad. Life was very chaotic. All three of us boys played multiple sports. At minimum we participated in football, baseball, and wrestling every year. Sometimes we added in track, soccer and basketball. Every once in a while we would double up and play two sports at one time.

It is important you also know we are ten years apart from the first born to the baby. For almost twenty-nine years, my mother traveled from practice to games to practice to games all the while teaching eighth grade math in a public school. My mother had to play many different roles in our life: teacher, preacher, pitcher, catcher, counselor, consoler, educator, doctor, judge, jury, and executioner! If I could say anything about my mother it would be that she was consistent in the chaos.

Motherhood was no different for Mary, the mother of Jesus. Mary was living a simple, small-town life, when everything suddenly changed. She was shoved from the shadows into the spotlight when an angel appeared to her out of nowhere and said, "Do not be afraid, Mary; you have found favor with God. You will conceive and give birth to a son, and you are to call him Jesus. He will be great and will be called the Son of the Most High. The Lord God will give him the throne of his father David, and he will reign over Jacob's descendants forever; his kingdom will never end." (Luke 1:30-33) NIV

You're Pregnant!

Two little words can change your life forever—"You're pregnant." Once you hear them, life is never the same. Imagine the shock when Mary was told she would be pregnant. Most scholars believe she was between the ages of thirteen and fifteen. And let's not forget she had never been with a man, at least not in the biblical sense.

The only words she could manage to say were, "How can this be?"

Isn't that a logical question? I think I would have had a lot more to say than that!

She must have been terribly overwhelmed.

How was she going to explain this to her parents? Um. Mom. Dad. I'm pregnant. But great news. It's God's baby.

How would she explain this to Joseph? "Um, Joe. I love you. But I need to tell you something. I'm about to be God's baby mama."

How would she explain this to the church? Good news everyone! You get to throw a baby shower for the long awaited Messiah!

You know the prayer chain was about to be blown up to a whole notha' level!

Let's not forget about the community? The looks she would have gotten. You know they would have disgusted the devil himself.

Mama DG

My mother got pregnant while in high school. She had her hopes and dreams. Her future was bright, but everything changed the moment she heard the words, "You're Pregnant." I once asked her about the shame she must have felt. Let's just say those closest to you are often the meanest. And the church people…they're too smart to shame you openly, they do it subtly. In the South, church women don't gossip, they just say, "Bless Your Heart." She received a lot of, "Bless Your Hearts."

There was a logical explanation for my mother's pregnancy. (If you don't know, ask your pastor; this isn't that kind of book.) Mary's only explanation was, "God got me pregnant!" Talk about conflict.

Who would believe her?

Joseph didn't. He was ready to send her packing.

Her parents may have even kicked her out of the house. Luke tells us Mary hurried out of town and ran to the hill country of Judea. She spent the next three months there.

Life couldn't get any more conflicted.

The Day Everything Changed

My wife and I planned the birth of our first child. At least we thought we had.

When Amy and I got married I told her I wanted to wait four years before we got pregnant. (Why do men say "we?" We are never pregnant. We do the easy part and have fun doing it. Again, if you don't know what that means ask your pastor; he would love to tell you how this happens.) Everything went according to plan. Amy got pregnant at the four year mark and we were good to go for a summer baby. We had a plan in place and it was a good plan. She taught school and we knew she would be out for summer break, so we planned accordingly. The last day of school was May 24 and the baby was due on June 6. This was too easy.

It is important you know my wife is a wonderful woman. The best person I have ever met. She is also a true southern belle. She is sexy, strong and stubborn! Seasoned with grace and grit.

For the first eight months of her pregnancy everything went perfectly. She never had morning sickness, never had a complication, and never missed one day of work. My wife taught school for nine years and never missed a day. Did I mention she is as tough as an old leather boot?

On May 17, three weeks before her due date, everything changed. Now up until this point, I had only gone to two appointments with her. The first was to find out if she was really pregnant, and the second was to find out if it was a boy or girl. My wife may be a southern belle, but I am a southern bull…stupid and insensitive.

That morning Amy got ready for school as normal. I don't remember everything she said that morning, but I do remember her telling me she wasn't feeling well. I said to her, "It's probably morning sickness. I've heard about it being a real thing. Go ahead and go to work. You'll be fine." Did I mention I wasn't very smart or sensitive? I knew she had a regularly scheduled appointment that afternoon so I figured she could make it until then. Apparently, I thought I was a pastor and a doctor.

Why do all men assume everyone will be fine without going to the doctor, except them?

"You'll be okay honey, it's just a virus. Take a Tylenol and a nap and you'll feel better in the morning."

But when we are sick, no one has ever been as sick as we are. In fact, we think we contracted something no one has even had before. It's so deadly I need my wife to wait on me hand and foot. I know my temperature is only ninety-nine degrees, but I may not live to see tomorrow.

You know I am speaking the truth. Men are big babies when they are sick.

It just so happened to be a Monday. As a pastor, I normally took Mondays off, so about noon I was lying on the couch watching my favorite daytime programming, *All My Children*, (please don't tell anyone), when she came walking through the door. I asked what she was doing home and she replied she came home sick. She wanted to lie down and rest before her appointment. Again, according to my medical opinion, it was probably just morning sickness. I read about such a thing on the internet.

After her nap, I decided it would be best if I drove her to the appointment. Who said chivalry was dead? A few moments after checking in, the nurse called her back. I chose to stay in the lobby and watch ESPN. We couldn't afford cable at our house so I had to take advantage of this opportunity. If I had known they had ESPN all along, I probably would have made it to every appointment! Ladies, please don't put the book down. Feel free to use me as an example to teach your husbands or sons what not to do.

In the middle of *Sports Center*, I heard a nurse asking for Mr. Voss. I figured I better respond. By the look on her face I could tell she meant business. She said, "Mr. Voss we are rushing your wife to the hospital. Her blood pressure is 170 over 122. She has to have this baby now."

I looked at her and said, "She can't have it today, I don't have the room ready yet. Besides, we still have three more weeks."

She replied, "If we don't get her to the hospital soon she is going to have a stroke and you will lose both her and your son."

I said, "Okay, I'll drive her."

Amy probably would have killed me had she had the strength. I literally refused an ambulance and insisted I drive her myself. What in the world was I thinking?

As we pulled up to the emergency room a set of nurses were already waiting for us. They were prepared for her arrival and they immediately rushed her back to prep for surgery. I was left in the lobby to fill out a few pages of paperwork. I'm pretty sure the nurses were plotting my death because the doctor's office had already called and warned them of my stupidity. They weren't very nice, but who could blame them?

After completing the appropriate paperwork, the nurse escorted me to a back room. Shortly thereafter, they brought Amy in for a few moments while they prepared the delivery room. What happened next was like a scene out of a horror movie. Paul did say, "God is not mocked, a man reaps what he sows." So I guess I had it coming.

The nurse assigned to us was a rookie. And when I say rookie, I mean it was her first day on the job. I don't know why she was given the task of inserting the IV into Amy's arm but she was. As you can tell, I am not a medical doctor nor a nurse, but isn't this one of the first things you learn before being allowed to work with patients? Apparently not, because this woman had no clue what she was doing. Fortunately for Amy, she was already heavily medicated.

The nurse tried everything to get the IV in Amy's arm, but it wasn't working. At one point the nurse even asked if I could help. I actually tried. Self-appointed Dr. Dan went to work.

I was hoping I could make it up to Amy by saving the day and inserting the IV, but I couldn't.

I am not lying when I say Amy's arm looked like a pin cushion.

Finally, after what seemed like forever, the nurse got the IV into Amy's arm.

However, now we had a bigger problem. Somehow, in all the mayhem, the cord became detached from the bag and blood was spilling everywhere.

Then the nurse did the unthinkable. She literally told me to "put one finger here and the other finger there," to keep the blood from coming out of Amy's arm and the fluids from leaking all over the floor. It was pure chaos!

I guess the nurses station finally heard the commotion and called for a real doctor. Talk about a life saver. I had never been a part of anything so crazy.

After getting everything cleaned up and taken care of, he explained Amy had come down with HELLP syndrome. One of the only known cures this far in the pregnancy is to deliver the baby immediately. The doctor explained the possible risks associated with an emergency C-Section and asked if we had any questions. Amy said, "No." I said, "Yes, can I call my mother first?"

I was scared to death. I was confused and conflicted and I wanted my mother. I am not a mama's boy by any means, but when life is complicated, isn't mama one of the first people we call to comfort us? I called my mother and said, "Pray!" She did.

Thankfully, after giving birth, everything in Amy's body went back to normal. Our son Noah had a few complications in the beginning, but rebounded quickly.

After three days they sent us home. I had no idea what to do and Amy wasn't fully recovered just yet. So what did I do? I called my mama.

Mary, Mary

When life got really complicated for Mary she didn't see it as an inconvenience nor did she look for a way out. She saw her pregnancy for what it was—a gift from God. Even though I am sure she was confused and scared, we never read about her complaining. Instead, her response was one of obedience and gratitude.

Mary said, "I am the Lord's servant…May your word to me be fulfilled." (Luke 1:38) NIV

She then celebrated the news by praying one of the most beautiful prayers ever recorded. Theologians refer to it as The Magnificat. A song of praise.

Mary said, "My soul doth magnify the Lord, And my spirit hath rejoiced in God my Savior. For he hath regarded the low estate of his handmaiden: for, behold, from henceforth all generations shall call me blessed. For he that is mighty hath done to me great things; and holy is his name." (Luke 1:46-49) KJV

In the middle of the chaos, in the middle of the conflict, in the middle of her confusion, she celebrated the fact that her child was a gift from God.

I wonder about you. How do you see your children? A reason to complain or a reason to celebrate? Sure, it's chaotic, but do your children know they are a treasured gift? When was the last time you told them how grateful and thankful you are for them? Do they hear more complaining or celebrating from your lips? Our words are prophecies over our children. So please choose your words wisely.

Maybe you don't have children. Maybe it's a job that is conflicting. Maybe it's a relationship that doesn't make sense. Maybe you received unexpected news.

Regardless of what it is, how do you react in situations that are beyond your control? Do you respond with criticism? Constantly critiquing those around you? Do you cast blame? Do you look for the easy way out? Do you run and hide, ignoring the pain that is there?

I know you are facing situations you did not choose, but you still get to make a choice. You choose your reaction. How you respond today determines how you live tomorrow. Mary made the choice to rejoice because that was the one thing she could control. The same is true for you. If you want to have joy no matter what happens on the journey, you need to always make the choice to rejoice.

Please understand, you cannot control what happens to you but you always get to make a choice. This is one of the greatest gifts God gives to us.

Bad to Worse

Unfortunately, the chaos was just getting started. A decree was issued that everyone should return to their hometown to be taxed.

So Joseph also went up from the town of Nazareth in Galilee to Judea, to Bethlehem the town of David, because he belonged to the house and line of David. He went there to register with Mary, who was pledged to be married to him and was expecting a child. While they were there, the time came for the baby to be born, and she gave birth to her firstborn, a son. She wrapped him in cloths and placed him in a manger, because there was no guest room available for them. (Luke 2:4-7) NIV

What do you do when favor wears the clothes of frustration adorned with the jewelry of failure?

Luke's Gospel says the angel pronounced Mary was highly favored. If she was so favored, then why is she pregnant on the back of a donkey, being led by a man who doubted her story, through the desert, traveling some seventy to eighty miles to look for any place to give birth to the Holy Child?

This was not an easy journey. They would have to travel south along the flatlands of the Jordan River, then west over the hills surrounding Jerusalem, and on to Bethlehem. It was a very grueling trip. The journey through the Judean Desert would have probably taken place during the winter, when it's in the thirties during the day and below freezing at night. It's a nasty, miserable time of year. The unpaved, hilly terrain and harsh weather were not the only hazards Joseph and Mary would have faced on their journey. One of the most terrifying dangers in ancient Palestine was the heavily forested valley of the Jordan River. Lions, bears and wild boars lived in the woods, as well as bandits and robbers.

The hardships did not end when they arrived in Bethlehem. The only place they could find to give birth to the Holy Child was a place where animals lived.

It's Complicated

Life is complicated. Things don't always go according to plan. Decisions are not always black or white, right or wrong, predictable or understandable. We are often conflicted as to what to do.

I'm strong, but I acted weak. I love my child, but I spoke in hate. I'm patient, but I reacted in anger. I'm wise, but I looked foolish. I'm compassionate, but I let passion take over.

If Mary teaches us anything it is how to be consistent when life is complicated. How to be steadfast when struggling. How to be faithful when frustrated. How to be purposeful even when you are pondering what in the world is going on.

Christ was born in a messy relationship, to a couple on the run who didn't have enough money to buy baby clothes. So Mary did the only thing she knew to do. She wrapped the Savior of the World in sour milk rags lying in a barn.

She shows us you can have favor, but still have fear.

You can have faith dripping off you like sweat and still have frustrations.

Such is the story of Mary.

She had a visitation from an angel but still didn't have a place to stay. She had the Holy Ghost come upon her but still had to ride on a donkey. What was within her was conceived by God Himself, but what came against her was demonic.

Our job is to be consistent in the chaos.

To stand even when you don't understand.

That's what Mary did.

If giving birth in a barn wasn't bad enough, she now had to run for her life.

After receiving gifts from the wise men, an angel appeared to Joseph and said, "Get up. Take the child and his mother and escape to Egypt. Stay there until I tell you, for Herod is going to search for the child to kill him." So he got up, took the child and his mother during the night and left for Egypt. (Matthew 2:13-14) NIV

She has a child she can't show off and a husband she hasn't been able to enjoy. A child who is different, parents who don't believe her, in-laws whom I'm positive don't like her, and a church who most likely ostracized her.

She has a son born from above but spends his first few years of life on the run.

Highly favored but going through hell.

I'm sure she's tired, lonely and disappointed.

It's conflicting.

Will I keep standing even when I don't have understanding?

Will I keep the faith even though I am frustrated?

Will I keep believing I am highly favored even though I feel like a failure?

The Bible says, "But Mary treasured up all these things and pondered them in her heart." (Luke 2:19) NIV

I may be sick, but.

I may have been hurt, but.

I didn't get the job I wanted, but.

I wasn't born into the right family, but.

I don't have an education, but.

I am not as talented as them, but.

My children are going crazy, but.

My bank account is on life support, but.

They just repossessed my car, but.

I just lost my job, but.

My spouse just served me with divorce papers, but.

"But Mary quietly pondered these things in her heart…"

The Greek word ponder means "an intense, protective keeping."

She protected her son as much as she could, but there came a day when she could no longer protect him.

She Lost Who?

In Luke 2 Jesus and his family made their annual pilgrimage to Jerusalem. It was something most Hebrew families did each year for Passover. When it was time for the family to leave after the seven day festival, Jesus decided to stay behind, without telling His parents. At the end of the day they noticed their twelve year old boy wasn't with them.

She had taken God's son to the busiest city in the world and lost him. There were no AMBER Alerts to sound, no public sirens to ring, and no news stations to beckon. She had no choice, but to turn around and head back into the city. For three days she yelled, "Jesus, Jesus, Jesus! Has anyone seen my little boy Jesus?"

Any parent who has lost their child in a crowded store knows the panic Mary felt. There is no greater sense of desperation and fear than losing a child.

Favored. Frustrated. Afraid. Now add failure.

When they finally found Jesus, He was in the Temple. Rather than apologizing for scaring the life out of Mary, His response was, "Why are you searching for me? Didn't you know I had to be about my Father's business?"

Parenting is complicated.

Motherhood is conflicting.

Even though He was right to serve His Heavenly Father, what He did to His earthly mother was wasn't right.

It's not easy being a parent. It's a lifetime of service training a young boy to become a man or young girl to become a woman. Then one day you have to let them go, and when you do, you have no idea which direction they will decide to go.

Eventually They All Grow Up

Jesus followed in His earthly father's footsteps for thirty years as a carpenter.

One day it all changed.

At the wedding in Cana of Galilee, Mary knew His time had come.

There comes a time when every parent must push the eagle out of the nest. For thirty years she had done her best to protect Him. Now the time had come to empower Him. She knew it was time for His purpose to be revealed. So she told the servants to do whatever He told them, thus pushing Him into His ministry. What she didn't know was this was the beginning of the end of the relationship she once had with her first born son. From this moment on, Jesus would be on a journey toward the cross.

The Gospels tell us that Jesus traveled around the area performing miracles. He healed the sick, raised the dead, made the lame walk and the mute talk. The leaders began to balk. They began to harass Him and rumors spread that they would arrest Him.

Then Jesus' mother and brothers arrived. Standing outside, they sent someone in to call Him. A crowd was sitting around Him, and they told Him, "Your mother and brothers are outside looking for you." "Who are my mother and my brothers?" he asked. Then He looked at those seated in a circle around Him and said, "Here are my mother and my brothers! Whoever does God's will is my brother and sister and mother." (Mark 3:31-35) NIV

The woman who raised Him, who suffered for Him, was rejected for Him, is now being rejected by Him?

It's conflicting.

She threw every birthday party and listened to every problem.

From the blessings of infancy to the burdens of adolescence.

From Bethlehem, to Egypt, to Nazareth, to Cana, it's always been about Him.

Now she's standing on the outside wanting to see Him and He won't take the time to talk with her.

Favored, but frustrated.

She spent her youth providing for Him, protecting Him, and picking up after Him. She went to every event, she washed every shirt, she made every meal. And now He doesn't acknowledge her? He even has the nerve to ask, "Who is my mother?"

Stand By Me

Her worst nightmare was now a reality. The son she pushed into ministry was now being punished on a cruel cross.

Imagine the memories that flooded her mind. From the angel's visit to the birth in a manger. From the wise men's gifts to Simeon's prophecy. From the Eastern star to Jesus' first steps. From turning wood into tables and water into wine. She had been standing there the whole time.

Now as He is hanging on a cross, John wrote, "Standing near the cross was Jesus' mother…Jesus saw her standing there…" (John 19:25-26) NLT

She didn't have to understand it all to stand with Him through it all. This is the essence of parenting. This is the essence of life. You don't have to understand it all to stand through it all.

Will you keep standing even when you don't have complete understanding?

Paul wrote to the church of Ephesus:

Finally, be strong in the Lord and in his mighty power. Put on the full armor of God, so that you can take your stand against the devil's schemes. For our struggle is not against flesh and blood, but against the rulers, against the authorities, against the powers of this dark world and against the spiritual forces of evil in the heavenly realms. Therefore put on the full armor of God, so that when the day of evil comes, you may be able to stand your ground, and after you have done everything, to stand. Stand firm… (Ephesians 6:10-14) NIV

I know times get tough. I know life is complicated. I know you are conflicted. I know you may not have the strength to keep fighting. I understand you might even be tired of praying. But don't give up.

Your kids, your spouse, your neighbor, your co-worker, someone in your life needs you to stay in there until the bad turns to good, the wrong turns to right, the weak turns to strong, the sickness gives way to healing, the depression gives way to hope, the addiction gives way to victory, and confusion bows its knee to confidence.

You are still favored, so don't let the presence of fear steal your faith.

God chose you for this assignment because He knew a lesser person would have caved. A weaker person would have walked away. A shallower person would have thrown in the towel.

Yes, you might get mad.

Yes, you might get frustrated.

Yes, you might even cry a time or two.

You might even want to throw in the towel, but don't you do it.

Keep loving. Keep praying. And keep standing even when you don't have understanding.

You may be in the hardest season and all hell may be breaking loose, but I don't care. Whatever season you're in, hang in there. God has you right where He wants you.

Keep standing whether it's going good or going bad.

Keep standing whether you feel like it or not.

Love until the love comes back, live until life comes back, and fight until everyone knows what you're fighting for.

If the enemy is looking for a runner or a quitter, he better look someplace else.

God trusted you with this situation so hang in there.

Tell yourself, "I don't have to understand it all, to stand through it all!"

There Was Something About Mary

Why did God choose Mary? I think I know the answer. When Mary went to visit her cousin Elizabeth, she said, "You are blessed because you believed that the Lord would do what he said."

Why did God choose Mary to have His Son? She simply believed God would do what He said He would do. If it is impossible to please God without faith, then it must be possible to please Him with it.

Through every circumstance, every inconvenience, or every look of suspicion. Through every trial and every false accusation. Through the crucifixion with tears streaming down her face. While her heart was breaking, she kept believing. Even when death rolled in and a stone was rolled in front of His tomb, she kept believing. She kept believing all the way up to early Sunday morning when she received the news, "The tomb was empty; Jesus was alive!"

I need you to keep believing until death becomes life again. I need you to believe in the promises of God, even when it seems all hell is breaking loose. I know it may seem like Friday, but I promise, if you keep believing, Sunday will come.

Be consistent in the chaos. Even when the tears are streaming down your face. Whether it be in marriage or in divorce, in sickness or in health, on the brightest of days to the darkest of nights, take a deep breath and say, "If Mary can do it, I can do it. Life may be crazy and chaotic, but if she can do it, I can do it. I may not understand it all, but that won't stop me from standing through it all."

You'll Get It Back

I love the last glimpse the Bible gives us of Mary. In the book of Acts Luke says,

"They went upstairs to the room where they were staying. Those present were Peter, John, James and Andrew; Philip and Thomas, Bartholomew and Matthew; James son of Alphaeus and Simon the Zealot, and Judas son of James. They all joined together constantly in prayer, along with the women and Mary the mother of Jesus…" (Acts 1:13-14) NIV

Mary is present in the upper room with the Apostles after Jesus' ascension. Jesus had recently revealed after His death He would send a Comforter. Comfort is what they needed, but what they got was so much better.

When the day of Pentecost came, they were all together in one place. Suddenly a sound like the blowing of a violent wind came from heaven and filled the whole house where they were sitting. They saw what seemed to be tongues of fire that separated and came to rest on each of them. All of them were filled with the Holy Spirit and began to speak in other tongues as the Spirit enabled them. (Acts 2:1-4) NIV

She was there when He was born, she was there when His ministry began, she was there when He died, she was there when He rose again, she was there when He ascended, and she was there when the Holy Spirit descended.

In other words, if you just hold on, whatever it looks like you have lost, are doing in vain, has forgotten or left you - will come back to you in a greater capacity.

Don't give up on your dream, God has a plan.

Don't give up on a child, God has a plan.

Don't stop praying, God has a plan.

Don't get frustrated, God has a plan.

If it all seems lost, hold on, God has a plan.

If all you do is stand, then I promise you, God will still fulfill His plan!

He is the author and finisher of our faith.

What God starts, nothing can stop.

Not even the devil or death itself.

So keep standing even when you don't have complete understanding.

Believe in the LORD your God, and you will be able to stand firm! (2 Chronicles 20:20) NLT

Increase your faith and He will increase your fortitude.

Sermon in a sentence: You don't have to understand it all to stand through it all.

CONFIDENT BUT CONFUSED

CHAPTER 2

THE STORY OF JOHN THE BAPTIST

What happens when the truths you believe collide with the life you are living? What happens when we pray for our friend to be healed, but instead the sickness gets worse? What happens when we pray for children to be protected, but instead they face abuse? What happens when we work hard, give our tithes, but instead of a promotion, we receive a pink slip?

Innocent people are still falsely accused.

Justice is not always served.

Good people die young.

Bad things happen to good people.

Everyone wonders, "Where is God?"

Is He sleeping? Did He clock in today? Is He on vacation? Is it His Sabbath? Does He even care? How could a loving God allow good people to suffer?

A truly loving father would spare his children of heartache.

If I saw disaster approaching my child, and did nothing to prevent it, you would lock me up and throw away the key. Yet bad things keep happening to God's children, and it seems the one person who could stop it, does absolutely nothing. Good Christians are not supposed to think this way, but we do. If God is good, why is life so hard?

When we have these questions, when God doesn't come through, or doesn't come through in the way we think He should, what should we do? I'm not sure what you do, but I know what most people do. At least, I know what I do. I doubt.

Have you ever had doubts?

Of course you have. With society changing so fast and the ever changing issues we face, this is the most doubtful time in history. I also know most of you would never admit it publicly, or at least not in church, because doubt is not allowed in church.

It doesn't matter whether you try to oppress, repress or suppress your doubts, all of God's children have them from time to time.

It may surprise you, but doubt itself is not sinful. It's what you do with the doubt that makes it sinful or not. Refusing to confront it may lead to the loss of faith all together. Whereas, for those who choose to admit their doubts and work through them, it may lead to their greatest moment of spiritual growth.

Doubt can actually help develop our faith.

I have heard too many pastors say, "Doubt is the opposite of faith." Doubt is not the opposite of faith. Unbelief is the opposite of faith. Unbelief is a refusal to believe, while doubt is trying to figure it all out. I would even go a step further and say certainty is the opposite of faith.

Charles Spurgeon, the Prince of Preachers, said, "If a man says he doesn't doubt, doubt that man."□

God never condemns His people when they have sincere questions, the same way you never condemn your kids when they have questions. If God controls the universe, which I believe He does, I think He can handle our questions. As long as we are willing to accept the answers He provides.

Paul told the church at Philippi, "Work out your salvation with fear and trembling." (Philippians 2:12) NIV

It is hard work trying to figure out life. Finding it hard to believe does not mean I don't believe, it just means I'm trying to work it all out. So when in doubt, work it out, and see where the real problem lies.

People ask me all the time, "Do all the tragedies in the world shake your faith?" My answer is always no. Does it hurt? Yes. Do I get angry? Of course. However, tragedy doesn't rattle my belief in God, it reaffirms my belief in evil. Tragedy reminds me what the Bible says is true. Sin is real. Freedom is a choice. Jesus is the only hope we have. Not counseling, not education, not bettering our economy, not more laws, bigger government, more therapy, or more enlightenment. Those things can be good, but they are not the answer for the problems of this world. Jesus is.

My doubt is in the goodness of man, not the goodness of God. Women will keep marrying abusive men. Children will be left in the hands of unreliable people. Adults will leave guns unsecured around the house. People will continue to drive at excessive speeds. Alcohol will continue to be sold at public places. Gambling will always be legal. Our government will keep making bad decisions. Advertising will always trick you into taking the bait.

The problem isn't with God.

The problem is with me.

The problem is with you.

Maybe the reason God doesn't answer the question as to why bad things keep happening to good people is because we aren't really looking for the truth as much as we are looking for an argument.

Could He ever give an explanation that would satisfy you when you lose a loved one?

The truth is, God created this world without sin, heartache, pain, sickness and death. We are the ones who continually bring these things into this world. The problem of suffering is the problem of freedom. Because we are free, we are free to make our own choices and with this freedom comes pain and heartache. What is right for me will eventually collide with what is right for you, and when that happens, one of us is going to get hurt.

Before we start saying God destroyed our perfect world, we need to think again. We are the ones who destroyed His. As a result, terrible, tragic things occur.

Didn't God create Satan? Isn't that creating evil? No. God created Lucifer, an angel of light. Lucifer, in his pride, tried to make himself equal with God. As a result, he and a third of the angels were cast out of heaven. His problem is our problem. We are prideful and selfish creatures, and bad things always come from pride and selfishness.

The Original JB

The Gospel writer Matthew tells us about a man named John the Baptist. John was born to aging parents, Zacharias and Elizabeth, who were of the priestly line. Interestingly, John's mother Elizabeth was related to Mary, the mother of Jesus, making Jesus a distant cousin of John.

John is about six months older than Jesus. He served during the inter-testament period between the Old and New Testaments, which makes him the last of the Old Testament prophets and the first of the New Testament pastors. The Gospel writers tell us people came from all over the region to hear him speak. As a result, many people were baptized by John. We also read he was a little eccentric. He lived in the wilderness wearing camel skin and leather as clothes, and chose to eat wild honey and locusts as food. He was the original hipster.

John proved to be an excellent witness to the nature of Christ. As he began to generate attention, a delegation of priests and Levites were dispatched in order to discover his identity. John emphatically stated he was not the promised Messiah, nor was he a reincarnated Elijah. Rather, he was the fulfillment of Isaiah's prophecy, "The voice of preparation for the arrival of the Messiah." He also went on to publicly state he was not even worthy to carry Jesus' sandals.

Jesus is quoted by Matthew as saying, "I tell you the truth, of all who have ever lived, none is greater than John the Baptist." (Matthew 11:11) NLT

Did you catch that? Jesus declared John as the greatest man who ever lived.

But…John has a question, "Are you the Messiah we've been expecting or should we keep looking for someone else?"

At first glance there is nothing strange about this question. An entire country had been waiting a thousand years for this question to be answered. Many people are still asking the very same question today, "Who was Jesus?"

What makes this question a little odd is that John had already declared Jesus to be the Messiah. In fact, he was the first person who publicly stated Jesus was the Lamb of God. He even went on to say "Jesus takes away the sin of the world!" If that wasn't enough, he then said, "I testify this is the Son of God." (John 1:29, 34) NLT

In other words, I will stand in front of a court of law and proclaim these statements to be true. I am willing to put my name on the line for this guy.

There isn't even a hint of doubt in his declaration. He didn't say, "I think, I wonder, maybe, or he looks like he might be." Nope, he boldly proclaimed what no one else had done up until this point, "Jesus is the Son of God!"

His announcement was backed by an experience. Matthew says Jesus asked to be baptized by John. As He came up out of the water, the heavens opened, the Spirit of God descended upon Jesus, and a voice from heaven said, "This is my Son, whom I love; and with him I am well pleased." (Matthew 3:17) NIV

I have a tendency to get chills when the band plays my favorite song or when the pastor preaches my favorite passage. This guy saw the heavens open and heard the voice of God speak.

He was so sure who Jesus was, he told his disciples to stop following him and start following Jesus. I've never heard a pastor send his church members to another church. There is no way that would happen unless you are fully convinced this man is the Messiah.

Make no mistake. John knew who Jesus was.

How does the greatest man who ever lived ask the very same question an atheist would ask?

I'll tell you how. Life happens. Life has a way of knocking your legs out from underneath you. Life has a way of leaving you lying flat on your back staring up into the heavens wondering, "How could a good God allow this to happen?"

These things shake us to the core of who we are and challenge everything we believe.

Not What I Expected

Have you ever bought something online? Of course. What about those Instagram advertisements? They get me every time. I hate admitting this, but I have spent way too much money on items I never use. Not a big deal in the grand scheme of things, unless you keep doing it. Then you have a problem. Yet, your problem isn't with doubt, your problem is that you have way too much faith in advertising.

We've all bought things that didn't turn out as expected.

Chances are you've also taken a job that didn't turn out as you expected.

But what happens when you put your faith in a person and it doesn't turn out as expected?

I've been hurt by people whom I really believed in, and when that happens, it hurts deeply. It takes a while to recover, if you ever do.

John had put his faith in Jesus. He, like so many others, assumed Jesus would make life easier. Instead, John is thrown into prison. He was an innocent man suffering because of the bad behavior of another person. As a result, he was confident in who Jesus was but confused in how He works.

From where he sits, Jesus doesn't look like the Messiah he envisioned.

Bad things are still happening to good people.

Evil people are still prospering while the righteous suffer.

The Messiah was supposed to usher in a new kingdom.

Things were supposed to get better, but they had only gotten worse!

Sound familiar?

I have been a pastor for over twenty years. Do you know how many people I have asked God to heal? Too many to count. Has He answered my prayers and miraculously healed people? Yes he has, but he hasn't healed every one.

When I was ten years old my grandfather was diagnosed with severe stomach cancer. They operated as soon as they could. Unfortunately, it was too late in the game. Cancer had spread all over. They did a few rounds of chemo and in a last ditch effort to preserve what quality of life he had left, they wiped out his insides, blew up part of his intestine to hold a little food, and sent him home to die. They said at most, he had six months to live.

This is when I learned how to pray. Not some little, "Now I lay me down to sleep…please heal my grandfather" prayer. I learned how to beg and bend God's ear until He showed up. My grandfather lived another twenty-seven years.

Do I believe God hears and heals? You bet. I have seen Him move in miraculous ways too many times to count.

Does it happen every time I pray? No.

I have also prayed for healing and the worst possible scenario happened. From my perspective, it seemed God did absolutely nothing.

In grade school a friend of mine had the most tragic thing happen to his family.

One day while playing in the yard his little brother was bitten by a tick. They didn't know it until days later when he was getting a haircut. Innocent enough. Happens all the time in Oklahoma during the summer. But this time was different. He didn't recover from the normal aches and pains associated with being bitten by a tick. He got worse, so he was taken to minor emergency and told it was a muscle injury. A week went by and he was fine. But then he got tired and his temperature rose. His mother took him back to the doctor and watched as they ran test after test. The doctors still couldn't find anything wrong so they advised giving him Tylenol, fluids, and waiting it out, so they did. A couple of days later he broke out in a rash. A return trip to the doctor still didn't result in any new findings, so they sent him home again. A few days later he couldn't use the restroom so they took him to the emergency room where he was treated for dehydration. The next morning he started hallucinating. They rushed him to the ICU and hit him with every type of medicine they could. The last thing he said to his mother was, "I'm sorry." It was the last conversation she would have with her four year old son. A few days later they said he had to be transported to a better hospital with the proper equipment to treat further. Two hours after arriving at the new hospital she was met in the emergency room by a chaplain. Rocky Mountain Spotted Fever had destroyed his little body and within a few hours he was gone. Did we pray? Yes. Did we believe God could heal this young boy? Of course. Did he? No. At least not in the way we expected him to.

When God does nothing everyone wants to know, "Are you the One we have been expecting? If you are, why am I still in prison? Why am I still in pain? Why am I still suffering? Why aren't You hearing my prayers? I lived for You, it cost me and it appears You are doing nothing."

May I Ask You a Question?

Instead of John getting bitter he decides to send his questions to Jesus. He didn't send his questions to a counselor or a life coach. He didn't send questions to his dad, who was a priest, or a peer who knew the Scriptures. He sent his questions to the only one who could answer them, Jesus. When the questions get to Jesus, Jesus doesn't give him a sermon on the goodness of God in an evil world. He doesn't talk about His sovereignty over all things. He doesn't scold him and say, "How could you John? Where is your faith?" He simply gives John the evidence he needs in order to regain his faith. He tells John's disciples to go back and tell him what they have seen. The blind receive sight, the lame walk, those who have leprosy are cleansed, the deaf hear, the dead are raised, and the Good News is proclaimed to the poor.

Jesus doesn't rebuke John, He reminds him. John, your perspective right now is limited because of the pain of your prison. I need you to look past the prison bars and see things through the eyes of faith. Your confidence is blinded by your conflict.

During pain and suffering nothing is more important than the perspective we bring to it. In the middle of suffering all you see is confusion and chaos. John, I need you to rise above it. I am not going to rebuke you, but remind you. This is bigger than you. Look at what I am doing. I am doing exactly what I was sent to do. I know you don't understand it right now, but you will. So I need you to look beyond your pain and see My purpose is being accomplished.

I think the problem with God always coming through for us is that we have misdefined what coming through means. We assume the only time God comes through is when He answers all of our prayers the way we want. If that is what we assume, He may not come through. If you understand that God coming through means He receives glory, even in the midst of the worst possible circumstances, and that He does all things for our eternal good, not just our temporary good, well then, I promise you, He always comes through.

This is where the beauty of Romans 8:28 comes into play, "And we know that in all things God works for the good of those who love him, who have been called according to his purpose." NIV

Without this verse, much of life doesn't make sense. It's like being given a bunch of puzzle pieces without the box. It is impossible to know how everything is going to fit together to make something beautiful.

Romans 8:28 promises that God will take every piece of our life and make it fit together in the most efficient, effective, and excellent way possible. It unlocks the mysteries of life. Sure, there will still be experiences that don't make sense until we get to heaven. Let me say as plainly as possible: there is nothing good about the bad things people do. Sin is sin. Evil is evil. If you have ever been the victim of injustice or betrayal or abuse, this doesn't negate that. It does, however, promise that God will recycle it, redeem it, and restore it for your good and His glory.

The key is recognizing the difference between immediate good and eternal good. Because if you are only worried about your immediate good, you are always going to be asking why bad things keep happening to you. You are going to feel like a victim and a victim always asks, "Why me?"

That really is the question, isn't it? Because when we hear of a terrorist being killed or a murderer dying in jail, be honest, we rarely question the issue of justice. In fact, I would even say most of us are silently thinking, "They got what they deserved." I expect bad people to suffer, but I don't understand why I do.

Can we at least admit that?

When we face suffering we have three choices: We can become bitter and blame God. We can become pitiful and throw a pity party. Or we can trust God is good, and somehow, someway, in His perfect time, He will take the bad and turn it into good.

That is what Romans 8:28 teaches.

God promises to use even the worst things that happen to us for our ultimate good. It doesn't mean bad things are good; that's sadistic. It means that no matter how bad things get, God can use them for good.

It certainly did for my community. We rallied around this family, drew close to God and each other. A scholarship was developed in his name and more people were made aware of this terrible disease. There's no doubt, countless lives have been saved as a result.

I know many people who have experienced the worst possible circumstances. Things that would take you to your knees in tears, yet, they allowed God to use them for His glory. Not at first. At first they were angry. But over time, instead of getting bitter, they took their questions to God. Have all of their questions been answered? No. Does it still hurt? Absolutely. But good things came from their tragedy.

Chances are, you have heard of MADD, Mothers Against Drunk Driving. Candy Lightner lost her thirteen year old daughter to a drunk driver. Was there anything good about that? Not at all. Did she get mad? Of course. Was she confused and filled with doubt? I would imagine. What did she do? She formed MADD. Since its inception it has saved thousands of lives.

Are You Offended?

After Jesus told John's disciples to go back and explain everything they had seen He says something that seems a little odd, "Blessed is anyone who does not stumble {or is easily offended} on account of me." (Matthew 11:6) NIV

Sometimes the way God works is offensive, isn't it? I don't understand why the evil prosper and the righteous suffer. I don't understand why my dad had to work thirty-five years in a metal shop just to put food on the table, while the adulterer down the street always had more than enough. I don't understand why my brother paid his tithes, was faithful to his wife and newborn baby, and lost his job. At the same time, his coworker never thought about God, never went to church, had the same amount of seniority as my brother, but kept his job.

I don't understand why it seems I have to work seven days a week to meet the needs of our church, when the guy across town seems to be on vacation six days a week. From my viewpoint, it appears I am working harder at building people and he is working harder at building social media followers. Is this petty? Probably. Does it upset me? Yes. Does it confuse me? Yes. Am I conflicted about how God works? Sadly, I am.

But at the same time I choose to have faith. I choose to pray and ask God to lift my perspective. I choose to believe God sees things I cannot see. I choose to believe God is bigger than I am. I choose to believe His ways are better than mine. Through the eyes of faith I choose to not be offended. When I have doubts, which I do, I choose to work them out. I choose to believe God is allowing something to happen to me so He can do greater things through me.

Maybe God is forging my character so I can stand strong in my calling. Maybe God is allowing pressure into my life so I can develop more power. Maybe the more pressure I withstand now will allow me to have greater purpose later.

If you look through the eyes of history this has always been the case. History is filled with examples of people who changed the world because of the character forged in the midst of the most terrible of tragedies. In fact, as weird as it sounds, almost everyone I've known who has gone through extreme hardships would choose to do it all again. Are they crazy? I think so. Or maybe they know something you and I don't. Tragedy is what led to their triumph and their strength came through their weakness.

Isn't that what the Lord told Paul when he faced an obstacle he couldn't overcome; "My strength is made perfect in your weakness?"

When you cannot do what you would like to do, God does what only He can do.

Paul went on to tell the church of Corinth, "Therefore I will boast all the more gladly about my weaknesses, so that Christ's power may rest on me....I delight in weaknesses, in insults, in hardships, in persecutions, in difficulties. For when I am weak, then I am strong." (2 Corinthians 12:9-10) NIV

Sounds a lot like saying, "I choose to be confident even though I am conflicted."

The choice is always yours.

Jesus' Best Man

After John's disciples left, Jesus said, "I tell you the truth, of all who have ever lived, none is greater than John the Baptist." (Matthew 11:11) NLT

This is important. Jesus affirms His faith in John, while John is doubting his faith in Jesus. It's as if Jesus is saying, "Listen everyone. John has questions. John has doubts. That's okay. It doesn't take away from who he is or what he stands for. He is still the best man I have ever met."

Paul says, "I am convinced that nothing can ever separate us from God's love. Neither death nor life, neither angels nor demons, neither our fears for today nor our worries (doubts) about tomorrow." (Romans 8:38) NLT

Did you catch that? Paul says he is convinced that not even our doubts can separate us from God's love. Doubt is not sinful, but it can be dangerous. It's what we do with our doubt that matters.

When in doubt, work it out.

1. Admit Your Doubts and Ask for Help.

John didn't hesitate to ask for help. Even though he was the forerunner of the Messiah, even though he was the first to recognize Jesus' deity, even though he was the one who baptized Jesus, he wasn't afraid to say, "Hey, I've some got some questions I need help answering." God can handle your questions. For goodness sake, He already knows you have them. Why not admit them and ask for help? My pastor always said, "You gotta admit you need help to get help." I like to say, "Own it to overcome it."

2. Act on Your Faith, Not Your Doubts.

There are going to be moments in life when you don't know how everything is going to turn out. In those moments, take a deep breath, place what faith you have in Him, and pray the most honest prayer possible. Even if it sounds a little like this: "God, I don't have much faith, but I trust you with the faith I have." Jesus said "mustard seed" faith still has the ability to move a mountain. Why did He use the example of a mustard seed? Because sometimes that is all the faith you have.

Faith is very much like a muscle. The more you exercise it, the more it grows. I have heard it said many times that whatever we feed grows and whatever we starve dies. Instead of feeding your doubts by worrying, feed your faith by praising God for what you do have. As you do, your faith will grow stronger.

3. Doubt Your Doubts, Not Your Faith.

Don't cast your faith away simply because you have doubts. For some reason it is easier to trust in your doubts than it is your faith. Why? Because most of the time your doubts are right in front of you, such as the pink slip, the divorce papers, the overdue mortgage, the late car payment, the scale. Those things never leave your sight. To believe things get better takes faith, and you can't always see faith.

In these moments, keep going back to what you know to be true: God is good and everything He does is for your good. He has never let you down before and He won't start now.

A few years ago the transmission went out on my 2005 Honda Accord. It was the most frustrating experience I have ever had with a car. My $3,500 Dave Ramsey special ended up costing me $8,000. Several times over the course of a month, the car was placed in the shop with one problem after another. Several thousand dollars later, I decided to get rid of the car and cut my losses. The entire ordeal was annoying and a major inconvenience.

Surprisingly, I never once said, "I am never going to buy a car or drive again." Why? One bad experience wasn't going to change my mind about driving. I wasn't going to take a moment and turn it into a monument.

I even went out and purchased a newer one, and made sure it came with a warranty. Sorry Dave!

I have seen terrible movies; that doesn't keep me from going back to the theater.

I have eaten at terrible restaurants; that doesn't keep me from eating.

Silly illustrations I know, but you would be surprised how many times people lose their faith in God or stop going to church all together because of one or two bad experiences.

Don't let what's wrong with the world keep you from remembering what's right about God. If you can't see His hand, trust His heart. If you look back over your life, you have to admit God has been good to you. Place your faith in His Word and in His track record and doubt the doubts you are having.

Sermon in a Sentence: Doubt your doubts and feed your faith.

DIVINE BUT DISCOURAGED

CHAPTER 3

THE STORY OF JESUS

Pastors walk a thin line when it comes to authenticity and vulnerability. People want you to be like them, but not too much like them. It's a very thin line between the two and I'll never forget the first time I recognized how thin that line really is.

It's My Story and I'm Sticking to It

I started preaching when I was sixteen. Many pastors have some sort of spiritual or pastoral pedigree. I learned how to be a pastor from the School of Hard Knocks. When it comes to being around pastors, I've never felt like I belong.

The family I grew up in was very much like every other family in the Bible Belt. We went to church on Sunday, prayed before dinner, and didn't talk about God much in between. Going to church was something we did but not necessarily who we were. Sure, we were taught good morals and principles by my mother, but that's about it. When we weren't working around the house or doing school work, you could find us on some sort of field. Whether it be the baseball field, soccer field, football field, or even a field house, my parents invested a lot of money in our athletic endeavors and as a result, we were pretty good. Good enough to receive a scholarship to college. Well, at least that's what my parents hoped.

Going into high school you could say that was a very good possibility. In my school district, freshmen were still considered junior high. It was unprecedented for a freshmen to play high school varsity athletics. I will never forget the moment my junior high principal called me into her office and said the high school athletic director wanted to move me up to varsity athletics. Our wrestling team was pretty good that year and they wanted me to be on the varsity squad. Moving up meant I would have to rearrange my schedule and attend class with the high school students. It didn't take much to get me to agree. Sure enough, I was able to make varsity and helped our team win the first athletic state championship in school history. After wrestling season the high school baseball coach also petitioned for me to try out for his team as well, so I was blessed to make the varsity team in two sports as a freshmen.

I have always been deeply devoted to sports. It was my first love. But something began to change during my freshmen year.

As a family I can only remember us taking one vacation - Silver Dollar City in Branson, Missouri. Any spare money or time we had was spent traveling to tournaments. During my ninth grade year I met a kid named Chris Presley. We became fast friends. Chris was unlike anyone I had ever met. He and his family went to church more than one time a week, talked about Jesus every chance they got, and genuinely cared for others. Chris started challenging me on my relationship with Jesus, and for the first time I started thinking about what I wanted my spiritual life to look like.

I soon began attending youth group on Wednesday nights and youth events on Fridays. I even started reading the Bible and praying regularly.

In October of that year I attended a revival our church was holding. I will never forget that "old school, hell, fire, and brimstone" preacher. They called him the Mountain Man. I'm pretty sure it's because he was as big as a mountain!

On Friday evening he began speaking, more like screaming, on the subject of Jesus' return. He started talking about this thing called the Rapture and a coming judgement. Then he said something that rattled my bones and sent chills up my spine. He said, "I think Jesus is coming back this year!" Did I just hear him right? The world was coming to an end in the next two months? Yep, because he said it again. I was petrified. (I had been baptized as a kid, but that was because my mom wanted me to do it. I had never done it for myself so I was scared to death.) In my mind I was going to hell and according to the preacher, I was going soon!

I went home and tried to sleep it off, but that night the craziest thing happened. I was awakened in the middle of the night by a loud sound, like a blast or a horn. Immediately my mind went to the trumpet blast the preacher had talked about. He was right. Jesus was coming back not only this year, He was coming back tonight! I ran to my parents' room and opened the door that led to their balcony. I'm not exaggerating when I say the moon was blood red, also just like the pastor said. Not only was this guy a preacher, but he must be a prophet too. I was so scared I woke my mom and said, "Mama, I need to get saved, and get saved fast!" She asked me what was wrong and I explained to her the situation. She did what any good mother would do in this moment. She said, "Go back to sleep and we'll call the pastor in the morning."

Did she not hear what I said? There wasn't going to be a morning!

She reassured me there would be, so I went back to my room and prayed my little heart out. Sure enough, morning did come, and she did call the pastor. Phew, that was a close one.

On Saturday, October 15, 1994 I knelt in my pastor's office and gave my life to the Lord.

Fast forward a few months. Another good friend of mine, Michael Boggs, invited me to a revival at his church. All good churches in the South hold two revivals a year. One in the fall and one in the spring. Most would assume I would have learned my lesson by going to the first revival, but I'm not as smart as most people, so I went.

In between the preachers shouting, spitting, ranting and raving, he stopped. I thought he was catching his breath or getting a drink of water because I had never seen someone so red and out of breath. Instead, he looked right at me and my friend and said, "There is a young man in here tonight that God is calling to preach. God has his hand on someone in here tonight and He is asking you to surrender your dreams for His. He is asking you to pledge your life to His service and become a minister of the Gospel."

I didn't know this preacher from Adam, but somehow he knew me. I have never been so sure of someone talking directly to me as I was in this moment.

That is, until my friend Michael Boggs held his hand up. That was close!

To think God was calling me to give up my dreams of becoming a professional athlete to become a preacher. Well, that would be crazy.

No one in my family had ever been a preacher before. We are everyday laborers - metal and wood workers, ranchers and farmers. Honest people trying to earn an honest wage and live an honest life.

Preachers Gone Crazy

What's with these preachers anyway? Do they all speak like this in revival services? I wasn't sure, but what I was sure of, this preacher was right and he was wrong. God wasn't just calling one young man into the ministry, He was calling two.

But for now I was off the hook, because it was my friend who raised his hand.

However, there was something about that night I couldn't shake. That preacher's voice rang in my ear for over a year. Deep down I knew he was talking to me. Every time someone mentioned a college scholarship all I could hear was the preacher's words. Every time someone asked me about my future, my mind would race back to that night.

Finally, after about a year of dealing with this calling, I surrendered my life to full time ministry on July 24, 1996. Where? Another revival service.

On one hand I was relieved, but on another, I was extremely nervous.

How would my parents respond?

How would my coaches respond?

How would my friends respond?

What did this even mean?

Did I sign up for life?

I didn't know any pastors besides my own.

I don't even know how to become a pastor.

There were a million questions going through my mind.

Do I have to quit sports?

Do I have to go to one of those weird places and wear a robe and chant all day?

Do I have to change my name to "brother" or "father?"

Would I have to wear a suit and tie from now on?

Is that how you become a pastor?

Seriously, I had no idea. I thought knowing what I wanted to do after high school would make things easier, but it didn't. It actually seemed to be making things worse.

Mom, Dad, Sit down, I Have Something to Tell You

First things first, I had to tell my parents. I figured for safety reasons it would be best to tell my mother first. I will never forget the look of disappointment on her face. I had upset my mother before, (I am the middle child after all), but nothing like this.

She was devastated. Is there anything worse than seeing your mom's look of disappointment? If there is, I can't imagine it. Before you pass too much judgment on her, think about what your reaction would be if you spent almost all of your free time and extra money on your child, hoping to set them up for success so life would be easier for them than it was for you.

Everyone knows pastors aren't paid much, or at least none of the ones I knew were. Life is difficult for a pastor. Besides the football coach they are the most scrutinized person in the community. Pastors live in glass houses. Everything they say and do is placed under a microscope. My mom was smart enough to know this. That's not the life she wanted for her child and who could blame her? She had plans for me. Go to college, play sports, get a degree, become Governor, and take over the world. All the normal stuff moms want for their kids. Why would I throw it away to become a pastor? Couldn't I be of better help to the world by running for office or by running a business or coaching a team?

Seriously, a pastor?

Yes, mom. A pastor.

I barely made it out if this conversation alive and now I would have to tell my dad. If it goes anywhere near the way it went with my mom I may not live long enough to become a pastor.

Late one evening I sat him down and broke the news. Of course my mom had already informed him, so maybe because he had time to process it, or maybe because he was numb to it, it went better than I thought. A few choice words here and there, followed by a few moments of asking if I was on drugs; then he was done. For the most part, they left me alone. Sure, from time to time they would casually tell me I could still go to college and play sports. No reason to rush. I have the rest of my life to become a pastor. They were right, but my mind was already made up. I would do whatever it took to pursue God's calling upon my life.

Hi Ho, Hi Ho, It's Off to College I Go

I decided to attend a small Bible College near Oklahoma City. They had a baseball program, which would allow me to continue playing ball, while still pursuing a degree in Theology. In April of my senior year of high school, I drove myself to the college and filled out the necessary paperwork to become a student in the fall. It was the very first time I stepped foot on campus. If I wanted to pursue this route I would have to do it on my own. In fact, the only time my dad visited was the day I graduated. If I was going this direction, I would have to do it alone.

The summer after high school I received an offer for a summer job at my church. It was not a glamorous job by any means. I was tasked with doing everything no one else wanted to do. When I say everything, I mean everything. It was my job to paint the classrooms, wash the buses, clean the bathrooms, and mow the grass. The church owned about six lots so it wasn't that big of a deal. The problem, however, was the pastor wanted to keep it looking like a golf course. So not only did I mow our grass, but I was also instructed that if anyone else on the block didn't take care of their yard, well, I would have to mow theirs too. Word got out and before long I was mowing the entire block, plus the center medians on the city's right of way! No lie. I mowed for my church, my neighborhood and my city. Talk about cheap labor.

Good thing Michael Boggs and I had started B and V's Lawn Service a few years earlier. It was God's way of getting me ready for church work. Do the things no one else wants to do, do it at a low price, and help the old ladies while you're at it. Pretty much sums up my lawn service and church experience.

I guess I did a good enough job because the next summer the church hired me as an assistant to the pastor.

It was trial by fire. The School of the Hardest Knocks. My pastor put me through the ringer. He had me do funerals and weddings at the last possible minute. I had to preach whenever I was told, even if that meant ten minutes before the service started. I drove teenagers all across the country even though I was still a teenager myself and had only been out of the state a few times. I was in charge of taking teenagers just a few years younger than me to hotels, ball parks, museums, and conventions all across the country. I don't know how any of us survived. I blew three motors in the church bus, spent the night on the side of the road several times, and crashed into a center guardrail just outside of Memphis. But hey, we had fun! So I guess I was a success, except when it came to preaching.

I didn't know the Bible very well, just what I remembered from Sunday school. In my first sermon I literally said Abraham sacrificed Isaac. I failed to read the entire story. When it came time for the invitation, I asked if the "magicians" would come forward.

The only part of being a pastor that was easy for me was the hard work.

At Bible College I was an outsider. I didn't know the spiritual "lingo" and my dad wasn't a pastor, so I didn't have the inside connections. It was like there was a secret society I wasn't born into. I didn't fit the mold of what it meant to be a minister.

I knew there was a divine call on my life, but I was discouraged. No matter how discouraging things got, though, I would not quit.

After graduating college I was hired to be the full time Youth Pastor at the same church. The only reason I think they hired me was for my lawn mowing skills. But a job is a job so I took it.

You Want Me to Be What?

A few years after taking the job as Youth Pastor, our Lead Pastor suddenly resigned. The church asked if I would be interested in taking the job. I have always believed that if God opens a door, walk through it.

It was the hardest six years of my life. People I thought were my friends decided it was best to be my enemy. Elders I trusted talked behind my back and worked against me. I have never been treated as badly as I was by some of the so called "spiritual leaders" of the church. My entire life was spent around rough unchurched people and they had more compassion than the people who were supposed to be leading the church. At least if they had a problem they would tell you face to face. Church people can be masters of deception; harmless as doves to your face, but mean as snakes behind your back.

Want to the know the hardest part of being a pastor? Being yourself and not being liked for it. Isn't that one of our greatest fears? To finally get to the point in life where we feel comfortable being vulnerable, and then to be rejected for it?

This is where I get the most discouraged.

Real and Raw

For some people, I may be a little too raw to be a pastor. I guess because of the way I was raised authenticity comes easy for me. If my parents taught me anything it was, "Be who you is, because you can't be who you ain't." So I don't mind talking about my heartaches, headaches, troubles or even temptations.

Remember how we started this chapter? People want you to be like them, but not too much like them. Where is the line?

One Sunday evening our Young Adult ministry was having a party. A few of us men were standing around talking about our jobs, our hobbies, our wives and our problems. I felt it was a safe environment so I made a remark that one of the guys didn't like. I didn't say a curse word. I didn't say anything rude. I didn't tell a foul joke or use offensive language, or at least I thought. It was what I would call locker room talk. You know, man stuff.

One of the guys took exception to what I said. He looked at me and said, "If I wanted that kind of speech I would have went to the bar."

I could see he was disappointed. Not sure why, but he was.

I was devastated.

He never came back to our church and I have never gotten over it.

Dis-courage

Discouragement is a very real part of life.

Have you ever been in a state of discouragement? I don't mean a moment of discouragement. For me, that happens every Sunday night. It's a running joke around our house that I preach to the people on Sunday mornings, then my wife preaches to me on Sunday evenings what I preached to the people on Sunday morning. Satan does his best work when I have been doing my best work. Crazy how that works.

In our last chapter Jesus was having a conversation with the disciples of John the Baptist. John's calling not only left him discouraged, but it left him filled with doubt. Make no mistake, he knew who Jesus was, but when you are discouraged, it is easy to doubt.

I need to back up and tell you the circumstances surrounding his arrest because they are more dramatic than the Jerry Springer show.

Herod, the ruler of Galilee, had an affair with his brother's wife and married her. John decided to confront Herod about his adulterous lifestyle. Naturally, Herod didn't appreciate this much and had John thrown in prison. Oddly enough, he kind of liked John; His teachings amused him.

One day, for his birthday, he threw a massive party. It was Jerusalem's Jammy Jammy Jam of the year. There were celebrities and coliseum stars, socialites and soldiers, governors and generals and girls, girls, girls! We get the idea - the party was off the chain. At some point in the festivities, the liquor started flowing and the king started talking foolish.

Alcohol never has anything of substance to say.

Herod calls for his niece, which is now his daughter. Told you it was Jerry Springer type stuff. His reason for calling her? She was beautiful and he wanted to show her off by having her do a little dance. This wasn't going to be some type of ballet dance. He wanted her to "dance." He wanted it to be sexy, seductive, and sadistic. It was dollar, dollar bills y'all! After a few minutes of shaking her tail feather and dropping it like it was hot, Herod calls her over and says, "Girl, that was awesome. I will give you whatever you want, up to half my kingdom."

Say what you want, but a grown man, a king, doesn't make this type of promise after watching the Nutcracker.

Being as young as she was, she didn't know exactly what to ask for. So she calls her mother Herodias for help. Should I ask for a new house, a new chariot, a prince, a thousand pounds of gold? Her mom said, "No. I want the head of John the Baptist on a platter." Um, okay.

I guess in hindsight who could really blame her? No one wants to be known as the town harlot, so why not kill the man who keeps reminding you that you are.

Herod had to be a man of his word in front of his boys so he orders for John to be killed. His head was delivered shortly thereafter on a silver platter. This is soap opera stuff; we have drinks, dancing and then a dead man's head on a platter. If the Bible is anything, it's real and raw.

After John's disciples buried him, they went and told Jesus. Jesus and His disciples were busy on the original Purpose Tour. They had been on the road teaching the crowds, healing the sick, casting out demons and raising the dead. Times were great. They had achieved rock star status. Everywhere they went crowds gathered.

Sovereign But Still Sad

It is important to know Jesus is the Son of God and nothing takes Him by surprise. Paul said He is the firstborn of all creation. He is before all things and in Him all things exist. Therefore, He cannot be shocked. Yet, for some reason He was taken aback by the death of John the Baptist. From all appearances, He is devastated.

Matthew says, "When Jesus heard what had happened, he withdrew by boat privately to a solitary place." (Matthew 14:13) NIV

Death and discouragement have a way of interrupting the best of plans, even if they are divine ones.

When pastors talk about Jesus, we love to talk about how loving He is, how merciful He is, or how compassionate He is, and He is certainly all of these things. When we say we need to become more like Jesus, we assume we need to be more caring, more patient, more forgiving and more peaceful. And rightly so. We do need to work on developing these attributes.

However, in this passage we are given a glimpse of what happens when Jesus' humanity and divinity collide. As a result we are given a unique look into the paradox of what it means to be fully human and fully divine.

When Jesus heard the news about John, He was devastated, He was broken, and He didn't hide it. I think we should learn a very valuable lesson from Jesus in this moment. Too often we go through hell all week then show up to church on Sunday and act heavenly.

When was the last time you just let yourself be sad? Seriously. When was the last time you went to your friends or your family and said, "You know what guys, things are not good. I'm hurting. I'm frustrated. I'm discouraged." When was the last time you came to church and when someone asked how you were doing you replied, "Not good at all."

Here's what I see every Sunday. The "Smiths" come rolling up to church. They walk up the sidewalk with their best smile and best outfits. Mom's makeup is nice and precise. The children have their shirts tucked in and hair parted over. After checking in the kids, mom and dad roll into the lobby hand in hand. They briefly separate so Dad can high five the brothers and mom can hug the sisters. They immediately come back together to show how much they hate being apart. Sister Flo asks how they are doing. Almost in unison they reply, "We are blessed and highly favored." Mrs. Smith adds, "I am too blessed to be stressed. This man of mine treats me so fine." Mr. Smith won't be outdone so he adds, "That's because she is so easy to love."

No one knows their bedroom is as cold as ice. No one knows they haven't slept together since they conceived their last child. No one knows she hasn't put on real clothes since last Sunday and her mascara has been running since Tuesday. No one knows she yelled at him in the car on the way to church and he cussed at her in the parking lot. Yet here they are, hand in hand, lying to everyone saying, "Oh, we're doing so good. Marriage is great and the kids are even better." But in the back of her mind she is wondering if she married Satan and if her kids are possessed. The only reason they are holding hands is because she's afraid of what he might say if he gets too far away. In fact, her last words to him as she got out of the car were, "If you tell anyone the truth about our marriage I will cut you with a knife when we get home!"

On the inside she is hurting so deeply, but on the outside she is put together so neatly.

I have heard it said, "You can't heal what stays hidden."

Jesus didn't try to hide His hurt. He didn't try to hide His brokenness with holiness. He didn't try to hide His sadness with gladness. He didn't say, "God is so good. All the time He is good." No, He was hurting. He had just lost His close friend and cousin. He didn't want to be around people because He was in pain, so He got in the boat and went off by Himself.

First Response

Think about this: Jesus could have reattached the head of John and said, "We good!" He healed a lame man who hadn't walked in thirty-eight years. He used mud to restore sight to a blind man. He had rebuked nature and defeated demons. This would have been nothing to Him. So why didn't He? Because that's not the way life works.

Life has a way of decapitating our dreams, cutting off our hopes, and severing close relationships. And when it happens, we need an example of what to do.

So Jesus doesn't say, "It's okay. John is in heaven smiling upon us. He's in a much better place now."

His first reaction is to get in the boat and get away. He wants to be left alone.

We don't know how long He is in the boat.

Maybe thirty minutes.

Maybe an hour.

Maybe two.

Maybe all night.

All we know is He got in the boat and let Himself go.

It might do you some good to just let yourself go. Admit you did not expect this person to walk out of your life after all the promises they made. Admit you didn't expect your spouse to walk out after twenty-three years of marriage. Admit you didn't expect the divorce papers to arrive on your doorstep so soon. Admit you didn't expect to have a miscarriage after you just painted the baby's room. Admit you didn't expect to say goodbye so soon to the child you never got to raise. Admit that after thirty-seven years of hard work you did not expect to be replaced just before retirement. Admit you didn't expect that after raising your kids in church they would turn out this way.

It's okay to say, "I did not expect to get this sickness after taking care of myself. I did not expect my friends and family to turn on me so quickly. I did not expect them to say that about me after all I have done for them. I did not expect that after paying my tithes for twenty years I would lose my house."

Some of you need to stop trying to fake it until you make it. You need to come into the house of God and allow yourself to break. The Bible is full of great men and women who were broken. Jesus was no different.

In His public sermon Jesus gave the Beatitudes. The very first Beatitude is, "Blessed are the poor in spirit, for theirs is the kingdom of heaven." (Matthew 5:3) NIV

Jesus taught from the very beginning that in order to get the help you need, you first need to admit you need help.

We have to be poor enough to admit we can't do this on our own. Let's face it, if you could you would have already done it. Life is hard. Pain is inevitable. Everything will not always be good at home. Work is going to be difficult. People will be mean. Raising children is crazy. We live in a fallen world and as a result, our hearts break.

The pathway to healing is often through our brokenness.

Jesus spent more time with the Father than anyone. He understood the ways of God like no other person who walked the face of the earth. Jesus is the Word of God and He was still wounded. He allowed himself to break and so should you.

The only alternative to being broken is becoming bitter.

Let's be honest, some of us are so bitter and as a result we have become calloused, hard and uncompassionate. Why? Because we see breaking as a sign of weakness, a sign that we don't have enough faith. So we quote scripture, "Though I walk through the valley of the shadow of death I will fear no evil, for thou art with me." Yes, that is absolutely true, but let's acknowledge the passage says we walk through the valley. Some of us will spend more time there than others, but every one of us will walk through valleys because they are a part of life.

Acting like the hurt isn't there does not make the hurt go away. In fact, it ensures the hurt hangs on.

Some of you are one dirty clothes argument away from becoming a single parent, yet you come to church, lift your hands, and then go home and want to hit him with a hammer. Nothing has changed. You thought your kids would bury you and you had to bury them. Guess what happens when you walk back into their bedroom? The pain is still there.

Acting like it doesn't hurt doesn't work.

It may do you some good to get in a quiet place and admit, "God, I'm hurt. God, I'm discouraged. God, I'm depressed. God, I don't get it."

Some of you reading this book are not good, but you keep telling everyone you are.

He can't fix it if you keep faking it.

I am giving you permission to get alone with God and cry. Go to your closet, get in the car, take a hot shower; let those tears run down your face and get to the throne of God's grace. Admit the situation is overwhelming and more than you can bear. Then, and only then, will He fill your hearts with hope and peace and comfort and strength.

You have been holding onto your hurt for too long because all of your life you have been told not to cry.

I am not sure if there are any men reading this, but if so, pay attention. If not, then ladies read this to your husbands. Too many Christian men are terrible husbands. They are mean and insensitive because they have never been taught how to properly express their emotions, and if they don't get the healing they need now, they are going to get old and crusty and push everyone they ever loved away. It's not a badge of honor to hold every emotion in; that makes us hardened. If we never express our hurt we will never be healed. If men don't allow themselves to open up and express their true emotions to their wife and kids, they will lose them. Maybe not physically, but I guarantee you emotionally.

So please let yourself go if need be. It's okay to hurt.

All the King's Horses

Let's get real. Some people have been hurt for way too long and it is downright disturbing.

The next story doesn't stop with Jesus sitting in a boat. There is a time to break, but then there comes a time to be put back together. You are not Humpty Dumpty. You can be put back together again.

Matthew goes on to say the crowds followed Jesus to the other side.

When Jesus landed and saw the large crowd, He had compassion on them and healed their sick. (Matthew 14:14) NIV

Don't miss this: He let Himself go, but when He got to the other side, when He stepped out of the boat, when He saw the people needed Him…are you ready for it? He got Himself together.

For everything there is a season…a time to weep and a time to laugh, a time to mourn and a time to dance. (Ecclesiastes 3:1, 4) NIV

Yes, there is a time to be in pieces, but there is also a time to be put back together.

Some people are a broken record.

Everything in their life is broken. Their parents, their spouse, the government, the church, the system, the pastor, their baby daddy, their thyroid, their back, their knees, their boss, their neighbor.

Blame is the name of their game and they have mastered it well.

I want to declare to you, it is time to get yourself together.

As a child of God we are not a defeated foe. He didn't defeat death so we would be victims.

Get yourself together. Stop blaming your boss. Stop blaming your job. Stop blaming your ex. Stop blaming your parents.

God does not put our destiny in someone else's hands. The broken record you keep playing is annoying. It's not doing you, or anyone around you, any favors; it's hindering your progress.

When Jesus saw the crowds waiting on Him, He got Himself together.

Please know, people are waiting on you. People are depending on you. Now is not the time to be out of control. Yes, your man is not here anymore. Yes, people walked out on you. Yes, you lost your job. But people still need you.

You can't keep mourning what you lost or you will lose what you have left.

Go into the closet and cry a bit, but when you come back to the kitchen, get yourself together. Your five year old doesn't need to keep hearing their dad is a deadbeat. They need to hear you say, "Son, we are going to get through this. We are going to make something of our life. God has something better in store for us. We are overcomers. Son, you are a child of God and you are going do something great with your life. You are more than a conqueror."

Yes, the door shut on you. Yes, the last thing they said was mean. I know it still rings in your ear, but they are not the defining voice in your life, nor will this be the defining moment of your life. They don't get to decide your calling.

Sit in the boat for a moment if you have to, but when you get to the other side, when your feet hit the ground, get yourself together because people are counting on you!

For some of you, the main limitation in your life is the broken record you keep playing over your life.

It might do you some good to thank God for all the negative people and negative stuff that left your life last year because all it did was make room for healthier people, wiser people, more encouraging, more positive and more caring people. Thank God for some of those people who left when they said they wouldn't; God was making room for more. Yes, you're hurting, but you're still here. Yes, you're in pain, but you still have a purpose.

Staying hurt won't help.

Yes, you were taken advantage of, but staying hurt won't help. I know you didn't plan on hearing them say that about you, but staying hurt won't help. I know you didn't get that promotion, but staying hurt won't help. I know you didn't plan on receiving that diagnosis, but staying hurt won't help. I know you lost something valuable, but staying hurt won't help.

If you stay broken you get bitter.

I heard Pastor Micahn Carter say, "Bitterness is brokenness left untreated."

If you are bitter, you start saying things like, "All men are dogs; all women are gold diggers; all bosses are jerks; all churches are hypocritical; all pastors are salesmen." No dummy, it's not every boss, every man, every woman, every church or every pastor. It's every you.

If you are bitter, the problem will follow you wherever you go because it's the same you that keeps showing up!

If you stay broken, you get bitter and if you stay composed, you lose compassion.

The Rest of the Story

Matthew goes on to write, "When Jesus landed and saw a large crowd, he had compassion on them and healed their sick. As evening approached, the disciples came to him and said, 'This is a remote place, and it's already getting late. Send the crowds away, so they can go to the villages and buy themselves some food.' Jesus replied, 'They do not need to go away. You give them something to eat.' 'We have here only five loaves of bread and two fish,' they answered. 'Bring them here to me,' he said. And he directed the people to sit down on the grass. Taking the five loaves and the two fish and looking up to heaven, he gave thanks and broke the loaves. Then he gave them to the disciples, and the disciples gave them to the people. They all ate and were satisfied, and the disciples picked up twelve basketfuls of broken pieces that were left over. The number of those who ate was about five thousand men, besides women and children." (Matthew 14:14-21) NIV

When Jesus stepped out of the boat He saw the crowds in need of help. Instead of asking them to come back another time, He had compassion on them and began to heal their sick. As the day was ending, the disciples told Jesus to dismiss the crowd.

Apparently, they were suffering from spiritual amnesia. They had forgotten what they felt when Jesus found them.

If you assume you have it all together, it becomes easy to forget what it felt like when you did not have it all together.

When someone is battling an addiction, you tell them to try harder. When someone is going through a difficult marriage, you tell them to attend church more. When someone is struggling it is easy to say you need to pray more. When someone is hungry it's easy to pass this off and say, "God takes care of those who take care of themselves."

Entitlement ends where gratitude begins.

When Jesus met Peter, he couldn't even catch a fish, but Jesus still filled His nets. Now Peter has the nerve to tell Him to send these people away? What you talkin' about Willis?

Jesus didn't send you away when you were hungry.

How about you Matthew? You were a tax collector, an outcast to society, a disgrace to your people.

Simon, you were a zealot. A silent assassin.

Thomas, we all know about you. You're a doubter.

And Judas. Don't even get me started.

What do you mean send these people away?

It might be good for you to go back to where you were when Jesus found you so your entitlement dies, your generosity is resurrected, and your perspective is changed.

Some of you didn't even have a job when God found you. Now you have a good job, a nice house, and a beautiful family. Some of you didn't think anyone could love you, but God gave you a loving spouse and caring friends. Some of you were addicted until God showed up and turned your life around. Some of you didn't know what was going to happen to your kids because they were hanging with the wrong crowd, doing the wrong things. In a last ditch effort you took them to church and they met some new friends. Now they love church and their lives are changed. Some of you were depressed and lonely, barely hanging by a thread. As a last resort you decided to give God one more chance before you took your own life. The moment you walked into church someone smiled at you, greeted you and loved on you. God surrounded you with people who encouraged you and accepted you. For the first time in a long time you felt hope. Your faith in humanity has been renewed. People do care, God is close, and tomorrow is a new day.

Yes, there is a time to let yourself go, but there is also a time to get yourself together. Lastly, there comes a time when you need to give yourself away.

Jesus was discouraged, but when He saw the crowds, when He saw the hungry who needed feeding, when He saw the hurting who needed hope, when He stepped out of the boat and His feet hit the ground, He gave Himself away.

Jesus showed up for the celebrations and the struggles.

He may have still been hurting, but He couldn't help, but help, those in need.

I know you're hurt, but people need your help. There are people in your family who need help. There are people on your block who are hungry. There are people you rub shoulders with everyday who are in need of hope. Jesus says, "I know you are discouraged. I know you are tired. I know you feel you don't have much to offer. But the pathway to overcoming discouragement is to offer encouragement. So whatever you have to give, give it."

I promise it will be given back multiple times over.

It's All I Have to Give

"They all ate and were satisfied, and the disciples picked up twelve basketfuls of broken pieces that were left over." (Matthew 14:20) NIV

Where did the twelve baskets come from?

Logic tells me someone brought them.

Either they were unwilling to share, or they came expecting to receive, thinking they had nothing to give.

One little boy said, "I know I don't have much, but what I do have, I am willing to share."

Isn't that all that matters? Sharing what we have.

What You Have is Enough

My parents were high school all stars. My dad excelled in athletics and my mother in academics. Their future was bright. My dad was going to pursue baseball in college and my mother would attend law school. Everything changed the moment my mother got pregnant. They finished high school, but their dreams of college were put on hold. Unsure of what the future might bring, they did the only thing they knew to do at that time; they got married and went to work. As you can imagine, life is not easy for teenaged parents, especially those who don't have any outside help. With little support from family and friends, they did the best they could to provide a loving environment for their newborn son. Scared and somewhat embarrassed, they started life together.

Shortly after marrying, they received some unexpected guests one evening. Members of a small church my mother had attended years before stopped in for a visit. There was no judgment, no condemnation; just love, support, and encouragement.

After the visit, my parents decided to give the church a try. Eventually, they gave their lives to the Lord. For the next year, a member of the church personally took the time to help my dad discover what it meant to be a man of God. He showed my dad what it meant to love the Lord, his wife, and his new family. My dad wasn't raised in the best of environments and had never seen what a man of God looked like. He didn't know how a husband or loving father should behave. If it hadn't been for that small church, that one visit, and that one friendship, I don't know where I would be today.

The men who stopped by to see my parents didn't have much to give, but they gave it anyway. They accepted my parents when they were hurting and without hope. They cared enough to invite them to church, to feed them, and to love them. Their small gift changed my parents, therefore changing me. And as long as I am pastoring, their harvest will always be multiplying.

There is someone just like my parents at your job, in your neighborhood, or in your community. God asks for us to find them and feed them. It won't happen if you have forgotten what He has done for you.

If you want to overcome discouragement then help others overcome theirs.

One More Thing

The prefix dis, means to fall out of, or be apart from. Discouragement literally means to fall out of courage. Encourage means to be filled with courage. Here's the good news. It is just as easy to fall into courage as it is to fall out of it.

On one side of the sea Jesus fell out of courage, but He made the decision that once His feet hit the other side of the sea, He would fall right back into it. Is it that easy? There is only one way to find out. Try it. Make up your mind today to be filled with courage.

God said to Joshua, "Have I not commanded you? Be strong and courageous." (Joshua 1:9) NIV

If it is a command, then it has to be a decision.

David also had a moment of discouragement. His men wanted to kill him. What did he do? David encouraged himself in the LORD his God. (1 Samuel 30:6) KJV

This may surprise you, but I think one of the most spiritual things you can do is to encourage yourself in the Lord. David said, "I don't have my friends, I don't have my family, but I have my faith. And if I have my faith, I don't need anyone to encourage me. I will just encourage myself!"

If David encouraged himself in the Lord, so can you. Don't believe me? Try it.

Sermon in a sentence: Let yourself go, get yourself together, and give yourself away.

BLESSED BUT NOT BLESSED

CHAPTER 4
THE STORY OF ESAU

Jacob, Jacob, Jacob! It's all about Jacob! What about Esau? I'm sure you have heard of him, but what do you really know about him? I would guess you remember something about him selling a birthright for a bowl of soup, but what else? Probably not much.

Esau always gets a bad rap, but I think he was set up for failure from the very beginning. His name literally means hairy. How hairy do you have to be for your parents to scar you for the rest of your life by naming you "Hairy"? His parents were begging for the kids on the playground to bully him. For goodness sake, they didn't even have to create a nickname for him. Next time just name him Chewbacca or Sasquatch or Cousin Itt for crying out loud.

Names are prophecies over your kids, so please name them wisely. If you name your child after a style or fragrance or brand, that style or fragrance or brand is going to go out of style. Your kid, however, will be stuck with the name. I know way too many kids who are trying to overcome the name their parents gave them. Jenner may have been a cool name back in 1976, but who wants to wear it proudly now? Just saying, your hero might turn out to be a zero and your kid is stuck with his name.

Bowl of Stew(pidity)

Most of us are familiar with Esau because of his twin brother Jacob. Jacob and Esau couldn't have been any different. Esau was a hunter and Jacob was a homemaker. Naturally, Esau was a daddy's boy and Jacob a mama's boy. As you know, when parents play favorites bad things happen. Can we be honest and admit we all have our favorites? I'm not going to lie, Noah is my favorite son and Eva is my favorite daughter. For those of you whom I just offended, I only have one son and one daughter, so relax!

The prophecy concerning the birth of these two boys foretold they would have problems. Their mother Rebekah was barren. Her husband Isaac prayed she would get pregnant. God answered his prayer, and she did. During her pregnancy, Rebekah sensed something wasn't right. The babies were literally wrestling within her womb. She prayed to the Lord and this is what He said, "The sons in your womb will become two nations. From the very beginning, the two nations will be rivals. One nation will be stronger than the other; and your older son will serve your younger son." (Genesis 25:23) NLT

From the very beginning we are told there will be problems.

Fast forward a few years.

Esau arrives home from a hunting trip. We don't know how long he has been gone, but it must have been quite a long time, because he believes if he doesn't eat soon, he is going to die. As he comes through the door in his hunting clothes, Jacob is cooking in his cute little apron. His stew must have smelled really good because Esau asks if Jacob would fix him a bowl. Jacob replied, "I'll give you some of my famous chunky beef stew if you will give me your birthright." In what becomes one of the lowest moments of his life, Esau says, "What good is my birthright if I'm dead?" So he willingly exchanges his inheritance for a bowl of stew.

Two questions: how good was Jacob's stew and how stupid was Esau?

As the firstborn son of Isaac, Esau was set to receive double what Jacob received.

Isaac was a very wealthy man, the son of Promise, the seed of Abraham. Abraham was the friend of God and the man whom God said would be blessed above every man on the face of the earth. His descendants would become more numerous than the stars in the sky and sand on the seashore. All of this would happen through Isaac.

What in the world was Esau thinking? Apparently he wasn't, because he was hungry.

Three things cloud the judgment of a man more than anything else.

1. Lack of food.

2. Lack of sleep.

3. Lack of intimacy.

A man has a hard time using good judgment if any of these three things occur.

Jacob understood this and hustled him in his lowest moment.

Hairy and the Hustler?

Isaac and Rebekah had a naming problem. Esau meant "hairy" and Jacob meant "heel grabber, deceiver." I like to say, "hustler." Can you imagine how this baby announcement went? Ladies and gentlemen, may I please introduce our new twin boys, "Hairy and the Hustler."

Fast forward a few more years. Isaac is getting older and his eyes are starting to fail him. He realizes his time on earth is short so he calls for Esau to pronounce his final blessing over him. Before he blesses him he has one last favor to ask, "Can you get me some wild game and fix my favorite meal?" Apparently cooking ran in the family. For his last meal he wants Esau to cook him some steak, ribs, mashed potatoes and gravy, okra, with a little banana pudding and pecan pie. He is a man of God, the son of Promise, and he wants some meat for his last meal. This is how I know I am walking in the will of God. My spiritual fathers loved a good barbecue too!

Esau agrees to his father's last request.

What they didn't know was Rebekah overheard the conversation. Remember, Jacob is her favorite son and no one wins when parents play favorites.

She tells Jacob to go kill two goats and cook them the way Isaac likes. Jacob is worried about the proposition so he says to his mother, "Esau is hairy and I'm 'Nairy.' My skin is silky smooth and his is rough and tough. What happens if dad touches my skin?"

Rebekah says, "Don't worry son, I already have a plan. We are going to cook one of the goats to eat and wrap the skin of the other one all over you." "Uh, okay! Whatever you say mom."

Jacob does everything his mother told him to do and now it was time to see if their plan worked. He brings the food to his dad. Isaac is a little confused about how quickly he was able to kill and prepare the meal, so he asks Jacob to come a little closer so he can touch him. He said, "Your voice sounds like Jacob but your skin is hairy like Esau." I can't help but ask again, "How hairy was this dude?" Really, the coat made of goat hair makes you say, "Yep, that's my boy?" Someone call Guinness because he may have been the world's hairiest man.

Hairy, We Have a Problem!

Isaac pronounces his final blessing over Jacob.

From the dew of heaven and the richness of the earth, may God always give you abundant harvests of grain and bountiful new wine. May many nations become your servants, and may they bow down to you. May you be the master over your brothers, and may your mother's sons bow down to you. All who curse you will be cursed, and all who bless you will be blessed. (Genesis 27:28-29) NLT

Not a bad blessing, is it?

As soon as he says amen, Jacob leaves and Esau enters. Esau has been doing exactly what his dad asked him to do. He isn't being disobedient. He isn't being rebellious. He is doing the will of his father. As he walks in the door and offers the food to Isaac, he is confused. "Who is this?" he asks. Esau says, "It's me, dad."

"It cannot be you. You were just in here. If you are Esau, who was that?" replied Isaac.

All of the sudden, his confusion turns to distress as he realizes he has been hustled. He had given the blessing to the wrong son. The Bible says he trembled violently. He explains to Esau what happened and Esau is overcome with emotion. Not only had Jacob stolen his physical birthright, but now he had stolen his spiritual blessing. He burst out in a loud, bitter cry, and begs for his dad to give him a blessing too. Isaac says, "I can't. I just gave it to your brother." Esau wouldn't take no for an answer, so he begs, "Please dad, please. Give me a blessing. There has to be something left for me."

Is there anything worse than doing everything you were asked to do, everything you were supposed to do, and not getting what you should have?

It's like going on the Whole30 diet. For fifteen days you are spitting out everything that tastes good. On day fifteen your friend says she wants to join. On day twenty you weigh yourself and you have gained five pounds. Your friend however, who doesn't even stick to the diet, loses fifteen pounds in five days! Frustrating.

It's like being married and wanting to have a baby. You and your husband have been praying, planning, and playing, but it's still not happening. However, a couple in your small group just got married, came back from the honeymoon and said, "You guys won't believe this. We got pregnant on our wedding night. We're not even sure we want a baby yet." You've been trying for seven years and these rabbits have been married for seven minutes and don't even know if they want a baby! Frustrating.

Single people know the struggle. You've been praying, fasting, grooming, exercising and starving while waiting for your man.

Then one Sunday, this new hot little thing comes rollin' up into church and starts talking to the man you have been praying for. Next thing you know he is buying her coffee after church! Frustrating.

Someone else gets the house of your dreams. Someone else gets the award. Someone else gets the new project. Someone else gets the position you have been praying for. Someone else gets the promotion you were promised.

Is there anything worse than doing everything God asks you to do and not getting what you thought you were going to get? Is there anything more frustrating than someone else walking in the room and getting everything you were supposed to get, leaving you with nothing?

I feel you. I really do.

Summer Intern or Summer Help?

For some reason, people think churches are just given to pastors. It might happen to some, but it didn't happen to me. I started at the bottom. And when I say bottom, I mean below the guys who showed up at the church as a part of the work release program. I couldn't get any lower.

I told you earlier, the summer after my senior year of high school I got a job at the church. Notice, I said job and not internship. The problem is, I thought I was getting an internship. You see, there were three of us who started at the same time. The other two got the title, "Intern," and I got the title, "Summer Help." Basically, I was cheap labor. The other two guys got to do all the stuff I thought I was going to get to do. One had allergies so he couldn't mow much. The other had fair skin so he couldn't be in the sun much. (Just kidding. Kind of.) That left me to do most of the manual labor while they sat in the pastor's office and chummed it up or went into the sanctuary and goofed around. It was frustrating. They got the speaking engagements, they got the opportunities, they got paid more, and they got to have more fun. They went home at noon; I didn't go home until dark. I was doing everything I was told to do and wasn't getting what I thought I should have gotten.

What happens when we don't get what we thought we were going to get?

I can tell you what happens to most. We start comparing and competing, and as a result we get bitter and resentful.

This is the story of Esau. His first reaction is anger and hatred and makes the commitment to kill Jacob as soon as Isaac dies.

Too many of us feel the same way. Maybe not to the degree Esau felt it, but we still feel it. They got what I deserve. They got what I should have gotten. They stole what was mine. We try to play it off like it's not there, but the moment we see them on Instagram, anger fills our soul. The moment we see them at the store, bitterness sets in. The moment their status on Facebook changes, jealousy overcomes us. The moment their name is mentioned, anxiety overtakes us.

I feel you Esau, I really do. All we ever hear about is Jacob. Jacob gets the new name. Jacob has the twelve tribes. Jacob meets the angel at Bethel. Jacob gets to see the angels ascending and descending heaven's ladder. Jacob gets the blessing. He also gets a wrestling match with God.

Can I say something you've probably never heard a pastor say before?

Jacob was a snake and it's frustrating to get hustled by a snake.

Sure, Esau made some mistakes…some absolutely catastrophic mistakes, but that doesn't take away from the fact that Jacob was a snake. He deceived Esau. Not once, but twice, and it seems he was rewarded for it. It's frustrating.

God Bless the NLT

I will never forget a message I heard from Pastor Micahn Carter on Esau. He read a verse in the Bible that I was sure he made up. It hit me hard. The truth is, I am like most people. I dismissed Esau after this moment; whatever he got, he had coming to him. It's all about Jacob.

When we left Esau he is begging for his dad to bless him. Isaac said, "I can't." Esau says, "Please dad, there has to be something left for me." Finally, Isaac agrees.

Listen to what he says to Esau:

Isaac said to Esau, "I have made Jacob your master and have declared that all his brothers will be his servants. I have guaranteed him an abundance of grain and wine—what is left for me to give you, my son?" Esau pleaded, "But do you have only one blessing? Oh my father, bless me, too!" Then Esau broke down and wept. Finally, his father, Isaac, said to him, "You will live away from the richness of the earth, and away from the dew of the heaven above. You will live by your sword, and you will serve your brother." (Genesis 27:37-40) NLT

Sure Esau, I will give you a blessing. Your brother will be your master. And not only will he be your master, but he will be rich and you will live away from the riches. Not only will you live away from the riches, but you will also live away from the rain. Not only will you not be rich and receive no rain, you will live by the sword and serve your brother.

Thanks dad, I feel so much better now!

But wait, he's not finished just yet. What Isaac says next is absolutely life changing. Please read it slowly, then read it again and again until it settles deep within your soul.

"But when you decide to break free, you will shake his yoke from your neck." (Genesis 27:40) NLT

Did you catch that? When Esau makes the decision to break free, he will shake Jacob's curse off his neck and be set free.

You see, it is the power of decision.

Jacob doesn't have any power over Esau that Esau doesn't let him have.

I want you to make that very same decision today. I want you to decide your future will not be determined by another person. I want you to decide your DNA does not have to determine your destiny. I want you to decide your mistakes will not keep you from your miracle. I want you to decide your brother will no longer be your burden. I want you to know that just because someone robbed you of a blessing, doesn't mean God won't give you another one.

I believe it's time to break free! Free from Isaac's curse. Free from Rebekah's neglect. Free from Jacob's deceit. Free from what daddy said or mama did not say. Free from what Jacob did or did not do. It's time to break free from your bitterness, bondage, jealousy, and rivalry.

It's time to break free and go get the blessings God has in store for you!

It is time to shake the yoke off your neck.

When you decide to break free, it doesn't matter what someone else got. It won't keep you from getting what God has for you.

When you decide to get over it and get on with your life, you will.

Their blessing does not have to be your curse. Yes, you got robbed of a blessing, but that doesn't mean you will not receive another one.

The moment you decide to break free, you will be free.

Your marriage will change, if you just decide. Your addictions will change, if you just decide. You future will change, if you just decide.

If you just decide, you will get your joy back. You will get your peace back. You will get your hope back.

So shake that yoke from your neck.

Whether it be a yoke of jealousy, a yoke of bitterness, a yoke of anger, or a yoke of hatred, it's held you in bondage long enough, so shake it off!

The moment you decide to let it go, Isaac says, "It has to let you go."

It is the power of decision.

This may be the only power you have over the situation.

So make the decision to let it go and take the power out of your enemy's hands. When you let it go, it has to let you go.

Player Got Played

Rebekah heard everything that Esau said and sent Jacob to live with her brother Laban, who had a daughter named Rachel. Jacob fell in love with Rachel at first sight. He asked to marry her and Laban agreed. But somehow on the wedding night Jacob was deceived into marrying her older sister Leah. Not sure how that happens, but it did. He was tricked into working fourteen years for Laban in order to have Rachel's hand in marriage.

Mama always said, "What goes around comes around."

Finally, after working close to twenty years for his father-in-law, Jacob decides to head back home. Problem is, the last time he was there, Esau promised to kill him.

He isn't sure how the reunion is going to go so he splits his family into two groups. Leah takes one group and Rachel takes the other. If Esau gets revenge, at least one side of the family will escape. He decides to send a group of messengers ahead with a large gift for Esau. The gift consisted of 220 goats, 220 rams, thirty camels, forty cows, ten bulls, and thirty donkeys. This was an extremely extravagant gift.

After delivering the message, the messengers returned to Jacob and reported, "We met your brother, Esau, and he is already on his way to meet you—with an army of 400 men!" Jacob was terrified at the news. (Genesis 32:6-7) NLT

Jacob assumes Esau is coming for blood.

Even though he's terrified, he sends the families on ahead. He decides to stay behind and spend the night in prayer. Alone in the desert, an angel appears to him.

A man came and wrestled with him until the dawn began to break. When the man saw that he would not win the match, he touched Jacob's hip and wrenched it out of its socket. Then the man said, "Let me go, for the dawn is breaking!" But Jacob said, "I will not let you go unless you bless me." (Genesis 32:24-26) NLT

Wait a minute. I thought Jacob was already blessed. He already had Esau's physical birthright and spiritual blessing. Why is he asking for another blessing?

Have you ever thought that maybe the person you are so jealous of, the person who got what you deserve, the person who gets you so angry and agitated, the person who stole your blessing might be walking in bondage too?

Some of you keep praying to be blessed when you are already blessed. You just can't see it because you spend too much time counting other people's blessings when you should be counting your own. Maybe if you started counting your blessings you wouldn't worry about everyone else's.

Just a thought.

As Jacob finishes his wrestling match he looks up and sees Esau is headed his way.

Jacob looked up and saw Esau coming with his 400 men….Then Jacob…as he approached his brother, he bowed to the ground seven times before him. Then Esau ran to meet him and embraced him, threw his arms around his neck, and kissed him. And they both wept. (Genesis 33:1-4) NLT

It's Not Supposed To Be This Way

Did you notice anything strange? Isaac said Esau would bow to Jacob, but that's not what happened. Jacob is supposed to be blessed and Esau is supposed to be bitter. However, Esau doesn't look like he is bitter and Jacob isn't acting like he's blessed. People who are bitter don't hug the neck of the blessed, and people who are blessed don't bow down to the bitter. Instead, Esau embraces the thing that should have made him bitter. In fact, he even hugs the neck of the one who hurt him. If you can do either one of those two things, it's a good indication you have shaken the yoke off your neck.

When you can buy baby clothes for the woman who got pregnant, the yoke isn't on you anymore. When you can throw a party for the person who got the promotion, the yoke isn't on you anymore. When you can pray for the person who caused you pain, the yoke isn't on you anymore. When you can bless the brother who hurt you, the yoke isn't on you anymore.

If you keep reading, Esau asks what all the gifts were for. Listen to Jacob's reply, "To find favor in your eyes, my lord." (vs. 8) NIV

Did you see that? He is asking for Esau's blessing and calls him, "lord." It was not supposed to be this way; it was supposed to be the other way around.

I love what Esau says in return, "My brother, I have plenty," Esau answered. "Keep what you have for yourself." (vs. 9) NLT

I can imagine Esau saying - Keep your pity, I already have plenty. I don't need what you have. I'm doing okay. I have my own blessings.

What he says next is absolutely amazing. Esau said, "Let's be going. I will lead the way." (vs. 12) NLT

This is so good! In essence Esau is saying - I know you're supposed to lead me, but I'm stepping back into my calling. I know what dad said, but there is another dad I listen to. My heavenly Father says I am the first born. It doesn't matter what Isaac said. It doesn't matter what Rebekah didn't say. What matters is what God says, and He says that when I decide to break free and let go, it has to let me go!

Open Hands, Open Heavens

I believe the way you let go of something in one season determines how and what you receive in the next. If you have not received what God promised you, it's not because He isn't able or willing to give it; it's because you may not be ready to receive it.

If every time "that person" posts on social media, you get annoyed, you're not ready. If every time you hear "their" name, your blood pressure rises, you're not ready. But the moment you decide to break free and get on with your life, I promise, God will be ready to give you your blessing.

There is no reason to walk in bitterness or comparison any longer. There is no reason to keep walking in frustration and defeat. God has more than enough to go around.

Tell yourself, "I'm about to be blessed and no one can stop it!" No one can stop what God starts.

Open your hands and let go of what you think you deserve and watch God open the windows of heaven and give you so much more.

On the backside of every, "no," is a, "you're next."

Things may seem out of control, but they are never out of His hands.

Just because someone else is blessed does not mean you are cursed.

Ready? Wrestle!

After working together that summer, my three friends and I went our different ways. Two of us went to college and one moved to Nashville. Ironically for me, I ended up getting a part time job at the church we, or should I say, "they," interned at. For the next two years, I drove a grueling 500 miles a week, to and from work, and on top of that was enrolled in twenty-four hours of classes each semester.

After college one of my friends started his own church while the other one traveled the country. Both experienced great success. Please don't get me wrong; they both deserved every bit of success they received. They are great men. But if I am being honest, it was very frustrating. I continued working at the same church for the next twelve years.

For twelve years I averaged over sixty hours a week. I was working my rear end off. Not only was the church suffering, but my marriage and my health were too. One day as I was walking out the door my then three year old son said, "Daddy, all you do is work, work, work, and preach, preach, preach." I was heartbroken. I was married to the church and separated from my family.

Inside I felt like I was dying. Pastoring this church was killing me. Yes, you read that right. It was killing me. The work of the church was killing the work of Christ in me. I was dying a slow death and no one knew it but me.

Looking back, I think God put me in that church because He needed to kill me off. He needed to kill off my pride, my jealousy, my comparison, and my bitterness. I needed to have my own wrestling match with God. I had to get over my frustrations so I could go get my own blessings. The moment you can celebrate those ahead of you and those around you, God will bless you. My friend's blessings were not my curse.

Make the Decision

I never got validation from my parents about my calling. Not even my pastor confirmed my calling. To this very day, I have never had anyone speak affirmation and blessings over my life like Jacob had. Sure, I get the obligatory, "great job," every Sunday, but I have never had anyone speak words of life over me. It's frustrating.

There came a time when I had to make the decision to believe I had value, whether other people validate me or not. Even if no one else knows my name, there is a God in heaven who does. I don't need the culture to tell me who I am because I already know whose I am.

I think Esau had a wrestling match with God long before Jacob did. It's not written down, but there had to have been a defining moment when Esau wrestled with his identity. He heard what his father said and saw how his mom treated him. He heard the prophecies.

We never forget the things our parents did or did not say to us, but at some point Esau realized it doesn't matter what someone else said. What matters is what God says. And I believe this is the reason why he was able to stand with authority when Jacob arrived. He no longer needed validation from another person.

If you are going to break out, you need to look in. Stop looking for external sources to solve your internal issues. We keep saying, "If I had someone to encourage me then I wouldn't be so insecure. If this person would have done that, I wouldn't be this way."

Jacob had the affirmation, but wasn't walking in authority. Esau didn't get the affirmation, but was walking in authority. Maybe the thing you think you need to get out of the bondage you are in is not in someone else, it's already in you!

You don't need other people to validate you if you know your own value.

Do you know how you determine something's value? By what someone is willing to pay for it.

Paul said, "You were bought with a price…" (1 Corinthians 7:23) ESV

What is that price? Peter says, "It was the precious blood of Christ, the sinless, spotless Lamb of God." (1 Peter 1:19) NLT

God gave His Son for you. Jesus gave His life for you. This is your real value.

Here is why this matters. If you don't deal with these conflicts, they will deal with you. Trust me, over time you will become bitter, critical, and jaded.

The good news is, the moment you decide to break free, the yoke has to let you go. And when it lets you go, you will finally be able to walk in the blessings God has for you.

I pray today is the day you decide to break free and shake off the yoke.

Esau got his blessing. You will too.

Sermon in a Sentence: The moment you decide to break free, you will be set free.

CHAPTER 5

THE STORIES OF LEAH & HANNAH

I will never forget Mrs. Nita Crain, my Kindergarten bus driver. It's not too often that a kid remembers the name of his Kindergarten bus driver, but I sure do. Every morning she would greet us with a smile, a hug, and a song. As we crisscrossed our way through the neighborhoods, and over the river to our little brick school, she would sing some of the most wonderful songs. Songs like *Zip-a-dee-doo-dah*, *Oklahoma*, and *Home on the Range*. I still remember it like it was yesterday.

One of my favorite lines from the song *Home on the Range* is:

Where seldom is heard, a discouraging word

and the skies are not cloudy all day.

Wouldn't you love to have a home where seldom is heard a discouraging word? How about a place where the skies are not cloudy all day?

Blue Skies Gone Gray

Recently my wife and I went on vacation. Every year we try to take a vacation and a trip. What's the difference? A vacation is just the two of us and a trip is with the kids. Anytime you add kids, the vacation is gone and the trip begins.

We decided to go back to a small resort in Playa del Carmen, Mexico. It is a beautiful place nestled along the white sand beaches of Southern Mexico. We love this particular hotel because it is unlike the others on the beach as it doesn't have the look and feel of the other big resorts in the area. They have done a wonderful job keeping everything looking natural.

There is something you should know about me. I like to plan and I like to pray. So naturally, months before our trip, I started planning and I started praying. The first thing I prayed for is not to see anyone I know. I know that sounds odd, but I want to be able to relax and not have to worry about anyone recognizing me as Pastor Daniel. On vacation I prefer to just be Daniel.

Amy booked our flight for first thing Monday morning. On our way to the terminal we passed a few people we knew from church. Fortunately, no one was headed in our direction. I was feeling pretty good about my prayers, when all of a sudden, just as I was about to board the plane, a Pastor friend of mine and his wife got in line right behind us. Sure enough, they were flying on the same plane, going to the same area. Now, let me clarify, they are wonderful people and for all I know, I was cramping their style and keeping their prayer from being answered. But seriously!

After a few moments of small talk we discovered once we landed we would be heading in opposite directions. Close call.

Amy and I keep a very busy schedule so our annual vacation is extremely important to us. It's a sacred event for sure. Not only do I pray for privacy, but I also pray for rest, romance, laughter, and beautiful weather.

When we arrived in Mexico the weather was absolutely gorgeous. After a short ride to the hotel we checked in and waited for the bellhop to escort us to our room. The resort was just as beautiful as I had remembered and things were looking good.

As we approached our room, I noticed our room was above another one. Normally, we reserve a private bungalow at this particular resort, but the one he was taking us to held two families. Not a big deal since we were at the beach and didn't plan on spending much time in the room anyway.

But…as we got closer it looked like my neighbor was sitting on the porch in a lawn chair, with his feet propped up on the rail, wearing absolutely nothing. I understand this is the beach, but I'm pretty sure, at least I hope, this isn't that type of beach.

Thankfully, he stood up and revealed he was wearing underwear. Although, I am almost positive it was the smallest pair of underwear a man can buy. Who am I to judge though? It's Mexico and he is on vacation. Whatever floats your boat, man.

The next thing I noticed was a row of beer bottles lined up from one side of the porch to the other. Take one down, pass it around, ninety-nine bottles of beer on the porch! This guy could hold his own in a beer chugging competition for sure.

I have nothing against those who drink, but I could tell by the look in his eye and the size of his underwear, he was there to party his week away.

But again, who am I to judge?

By the time Amy and I got settled in it was getting late in the evening. We quickly checked out the pool, the beach, and a local restaurant before heading to bed in order to make sure we were well rested for the week. After about an hour of sleep, Amy and I were awakened by a loud noise. Then another, and another. I ran onto the balcony to see what was the matter, when all of a sudden, I saw our neighbor from down under throwing stuff off the porch onto the lawn. He was yelling something I couldn't understand, but I could tell it wasn't pleasantries. For the next hour and a half he yelled obscenities, slammed doors, and tossed beer bottles out the front door.

Finally, about 3 a.m. security was able to get him calmed down, or at least calm enough for us to sleep what was left of the night…with one eye open.

The next morning we woke up to gray skies.

While at breakfast, we noticed the clouds were starting to roll in off the ocean. We assumed it would rain for a few minutes, maybe an hour, then roll out as quickly as they rolled in.

We were wrong.

Before we ended breakfast the rain had become a rain storm. Not just any storm, but the kind of storm Forrest Gump and Bubba talk about, "Little bitty stingin' rain, and big ol' fat rain, rain that flew in sideways, and rain that seemed to come straight up from underneath. Shoot, it even rained at night." Not only did it rain at night, it rained every day and every night the entire time we were there. Yes, I said the entire time. Now, I have a drunk yelling at me and rain soaking me. Great way to start a vacation.

As they say, the best is still yet to come.

After slowly making our way back to the room, we decided to wait out the rain by laying in the hammocks on our front porch. It never rains in Arizona so figured we might as well enjoy it. When life hands you lemons, make lemonade, right?

Well, before long, the wind starting picking up and I noticed it was starting to tear the bamboo shingles off the roof. I went inside to see if the same was happening in there. Instead, it was worse! The water was not only coming through the roof, but was also pouring out of the light fixtures and ceiling fan. I ran to the window to see if I could find anyone to help. When I opened the blinds, staring at me was the most ugly creature I had ever seen. It was the mix between a rat, monkey, and opossum. It was sitting in my window sill, licking its lips, just waiting to take a bite out of this country fried white boy. I screamed like a little girl. Sure enough, a maintenance man heard me and came to the rescue. He took the creature from the room but said I would have to wait out the leaks. Before leaving he said, “It is the rainforest you know.” I replied, “No, I didn’t know sir, I thought it was the beach!”

Amy and I patiently waited for the rain to stop, but as I already mentioned, it never did.

Thankfully, that night we had some more entertainment from our neighbor down under. It was man verses beer, verses chair, verses wife, verses porch, verses new swear words, and eventually verses the security. Finally, they were able to get him calmed down about 5 o’clock in the morning, just as the sun was starting to come up.

I briefly dozed off, but not for long because the next thing I knew I was wiping water off my face. The wind was tearing the roof off our room! Then I heard something. It sounded like an animal was in our room, right above my head, so I decided to investigate. I should have never done that. I should have just laid there staring at the rain imagining I was camping.

As I stuck my head above the ledge on our bed, I saw the most hideous thing I had ever seen. I thought the other creature was ugly…it looked like a puppy compared to this thing. I don't know how to describe it other than it was larger than a cat, had a long tail, protruded eyes, sharp fangs, and Freddy Krueger finger nails. I'm from the country and I have seen some ugly animals before, but I have never seen anything like this. I screamed, Amy screamed, it screamed, and the man from down under screamed too.

Miss Amy had enough. She marched to the front desk through the hurricane force wind and demanded they give us a new room.

Something you should know about Miss Amy. She is normally peaceful and quiet, meek and mild…not this time. I was genuinely scared for whoever was working the morning shift. She was about to unleash every ounce of anger she had been storing up for the last forty years.

After a few minutes of listening to her complaints and praying she wasn't going to strangle him, he promised us a new room; a room with a view.

We packed up our stuff as fast as we could.

When we got back to the front desk he said, "I'm sorry ma'am. The room won't be ready until 10 a.m." Amy replied, "I thought you told me to come as soon as we could get our stuff gathered up." He said, "I did, but I didn't think you would be ready so soon. It's only 5 a.m. and our custodial staff doesn't get here until 10 a.m."

I thought my little southern belle was going to unleash hell!

They promised to get us a new room as fast as they could, and they did. Four hours later!

Sure enough, the room was beautiful. It would have been a remarkable view of the ocean, had we been able to see it. The storm brought in so much seaweed that it not only covered the first fifteen feet of the beach, it also covered the first one hundred feet of the ocean. It was the most awful looking site you could imagine. If you think I am exaggerating, I'm not. This trip was quickly turning into the *Twilight Zone*.

Finally, after five days of being sheltered in our room staring at the rain, it was time to fly home. Our flight called for us to stop in Charlotte for a short layover before heading to Phoenix. The storm aided our flight speed so we landed an hour early. Now where I come from this sounds like a good thing, but apparently not. Because of our early arrival we were made to sit on the tarmac for an hour before a gate would open up.

When we were finally let off the plane, I could tell something wasn't right. For some reason, a reason not explained to us, TSA had shut down over 200 flights in and out of Charlotte. The line through customs was a nightmare and I figured there was no way we were going to make it through in time to make our next flight.

I was right.

Amy and I ran through the airport as fast as we could. As we approached the gate we could see it closing. It seemed to be closing in slow motion. We yelled as loud as we could, "Please, don't close the door! Noooooo!!!"

You know that wasn't going to happen.

Then to rub salt in our wounds, our luggage made it on the plane without us.

Due to the total number of flights canceled, there wasn't a rental car or hotel room available within twenty miles. The only clothes we had were the ones we were wearing and they were pretty much rain soaked. We were #nakedinnorthcarolina.

Mind the Gap

Psychologists say for most people the default voice in our mind is discouragement. When something happens that we did not plan on happening, our brain fills in the gap with negativity. In other words, Mrs. Crain and the writer of the song *Home on the Range* lied to me. We constantly hear discouraging words and our skies have seen a few clouds.

I can handle the rain. I can even handle vacations like this. Canceled flights? I'll get home eventually. Lost luggage? It will be found.

But what do you do when the days turn into weeks and weeks turn into months and months turn into years?

The truth is, my vacation is the epitome of the way my year has gone. Thankfully, I'm healthy, my family is healthy, and God is still good, yet it just seems to be one thing after another, such as loss of employees, loss of church members, loss of friends, and loss of family. New hires haven't turned out the way I thought they would. Old friends haven't treated me the way I thought they should. Constant gossip. Consistent questioning. Facebook lies. Twitter wars.

All of this leaves me tired, discouraged, and hurt.

Vacations are supposed to help, but often they don't. Friends are supposed to encourage, but sometimes they don't. Family is supposed to relieve the pressure, but often they add to it. God is supposed to answer prayers, but at times He doesn't. At least not from what we can tell.

These things leave us feeling discouraged. Almost like a dark cloud is hovering over our beach and doesn't seem to be leaving anytime soon.

Discouragement is something we all face. It doesn't discriminate and even the best Christians can fall under its power. I used to think the stronger I grew in my faith the less discouraged I would get. Unfortunately, I have learned the more you deal with people, and the closer you get to fulfilling your purpose, the more intense the battle with discouragement becomes.

If you are the one person who doesn't deal with discouragement, I warn you to be careful because if you haven't had a run in with the devil lately, chances are you might be running in the same direction.

Resistance is always strongest on the verge of a breakthrough.

If you haven't been discouraged lately, you are probably not doing much to go after your dreams. Everyone who sets out to do anything of significance will get discouraged. It's part of the game.

Mother of Discouragement

Quick question: Think of one person in the last century who has really modeled what it means to be a true servant of others. Think of someone who gave everything they had to help better the world. Did you think of Mother Teresa?

Listen to what she wrote in her journal:

"They say people in hell suffer pain because of the loss of God. Yet in my soul I feel the same terrible pain of God not wanting me, of God not being God. That darkness surrounds me on all sides. I can't lift my soul to God. I have no light or inspiration in my soul. I speak of the tender love of God for souls yet I long to believe it myself. This untold darkness, loneliness, longing for God, gives me a pain deep down in my heart. The place of God in my soul is blank. I feel He does not want me. He is not here."

Mother Teresa served God and her fellow man with all of her heart. Yet at the same time, dealt with discouragement the same way you and I do. Charles Spurgeon is known as the Prince of Preachers. He once said, "I would not wish upon my worst enemy the depths of despair and discouragement I often feel for weeks or months at a time."

We have this idea that discouragement goes away the closer we get to God, but some of the greatest men and women of the Bible dealt with severe bouts of despair. Yet, God still used them to provide hope even while they were going through a personal hell.

That's why I love the Bible. It always gives the entire story.

Growing closer to God doesn't mean you graduate from discouragement. It just means true joy is not determined by what happens to you, but by what Christ is doing in you.

Pastor Steven Furtick says, "The voices in our head are loud and constant while the voice of God seems silent and sporadic."

Wouldn't you agree? The negative voice in my head seems to speak a whole lot louder and more often than the positive one. I don't want it to be true. I wish it wasn't true. But it is.

So how can we learn to overcome discouragement when discouragement is overcoming us? How can we hold on to the promises of God when it seems God is holding out on us?

It Runs in the Family

I would like to share with you two stories: The first is the story of Leah.

Long story short, Abraham had Isaac at the age of one hundred. Isaac had two sons, Jacob and Esau. We talked about them in the last chapter.

Now let me fill in some gaps.

When Rebekah heard Esau say he was going to kill Jacob as soon as Isaac died, she deceived her husband into letting Jacob leave his home country.

Here is the best parenting advice I can give: Be who you want your kids to become. Every parent will have a legacy which is determined by the patterns we leave behind. You can have a good heart, but if you have terrible habits, your heart will not overcome your habits.

Let this sink in, "What does not get healed, gets handed down."

You will pass down to your kids your hurts, habits, and hang ups. If your kid is bitter, look in the mirror. If you kid is angry, look in the mirror. If your kid is a smart mouth, look in the mirror. If your kid is prejudiced, look in the mirror. If you don't get your act together, neither will your kids. Let me say this again, "What does not get healed, gets handed down." It will become a generational pattern.

Apparently, Jacob learned his deceitful behavior from his mother.

Rebekah deceived Isaac into letting Jacob leave the family based upon the lie of not wanting her son to marry a Canaanite woman. She sent Jacob to her brother Laban hoping he would be able to marry one of his daughters. Yes, you read that right. She wanted him to marry his cousin.

Remember what your mother used to tell you, "What goes around comes around?" Well, she was right.

When Jacob saw Rachel, daughter of his uncle Laban, and Laban's sheep, he went over and rolled the stone away from the mouth of the well and watered his uncle's sheep. Then Jacob kissed Rachel and began to weep aloud. He had told Rachel that he was a relative of her father and a son of Rebekah. So she ran and told her father. As soon as Laban heard the news about Jacob, his sister's son, he hurried to meet him. He embraced him, kissed him and brought him to his home, and there Jacob told him all these things. Then Laban said to him, "You are my own flesh and blood." After Jacob had stayed with him for a whole month, Laban said to him, "Just because you are a relative of mine, should you work for me for nothing? Tell me what your wages should be." Now Laban had two daughters; the name of the older was Leah, and the name of the younger was Rachel. Leah had weak eyes, (this is the Bible's way of saying she is uglier than a mud fence), but Rachel had a lovely figure and was beautiful. (Rachel is hot. Leah is not.) Jacob was in love with Rachel and said, "I'll work for you seven years in return for your younger daughter Rachel." Laban said, "It's better that I give her to you than to some other man. Stay here with me." So Jacob served seven years to get Rachel, but they seemed like only a few days to him because of his love for her. Then Jacob said to Laban, "Give me my wife. My time is completed and I want to make love to her." (Young men- I would not recommend using this verbiage when asking for your wife's hand in marriage.) So Laban brought together all the people of the place and gave a feast. But when evening came, he took his daughter Leah and brought her to Jacob, and Jacob made love to her. And Laban gave his servant Zilpah to his daughter as her attendant. When morning came, there was Leah! So Jacob said to Laban, "What is this you have done to me? I served you for Rachel, didn't I? Why have you deceived me?" (Genesis 29:10-25) NIV

Deceit runs in the family. Jacob deceived Esau. Rebekah deceived Isaac. Laban deceived Jacob.

The player got played at his own game.

This is why I love the Bible. It's better than the National Enquirer.

How do you think Leah feels in this moment? For a younger sister to be married before an older sister was extremely humiliating. In her culture a woman's identity was directly tied to being married and having children.

Listen ladies, the only thing worse than being single and lonely is being married and lonely. Let me give you some free advice: Don't rush love and don't marry your cousin.

Although it seems Rachel has it all, Leah is about to get the last laugh. She is able to have children and Rachel is not.

Leah became pregnant and gave birth to a son. She named him Reuben, for she said, "It is because the Lord has seen my misery. Surely my husband will love me now." She conceived again, and when she gave birth to a son she said, "Because the Lord heard that I am not loved, he gave me this one too." So she named him Simeon. Again she conceived, and when she gave birth to a son she said, "Now at last my husband will become attached to me, because I have borne him three sons." So he was named Levi. She conceived again, and when she gave birth to a son she said, "This time I will praise the Lord." So she named him Judah. Then she stopped having children. (vs. 32-35) NIV

Pastor Steven Furtick says, "Discouragement is the gap between what we expect and what we experience."

Leah expected to marry someone who would love and cherish her, but what she experienced was completely different.

All of us at one time or another will find ourselves in the gap between expectation and experience. And when that happens, discouragement shows up in a variety of ways. Sometimes it comes in like a flood, other times it drips slowly. It can come from others by what they say or don't say. It can come from events that happen or don't happen. It can come whether we are winning or losing, rich or poor, or whether we are a believer or non-believer. But never is it more on display than when we get married and have kids.

Not What I Expected

I didn't think much about having kids growing up, so I didn't have many expectations. But the expectations I did have were very different than my experience.

My son Noah cried for the first six months of his life. Constantly. All day, every day. We tried everything including car rides, soothing sounds, pacifiers, a bottle, but nothing helped. I would often hold him up in the middle of the night like Simba in the *Lion King* and pray, "Lord, please. I beg you. Help this kid stop crying." Many nights I think I cried louder than he did!

If the crying wasn't bad enough, every time he got angry he would hold his breath, turn blue, shake violently, and pass out. Every. Single. Time. We took him to the ER one night because we thought he was having a seizure. The doctor on call laughed through one of his episodes and said, "Looks like this is just his personality." Excuse me, what did you say? My son has a passing out personality?

I didn't expect much, but I didn't see that experience coming. He did this until he was four! After our third exorcism he finally stopped. Just kidding. Thankfully, he eventually outgrew it.

Expectations are a funny thing. We all have them and sometimes we don't even know they are there until they go unmet. And once they go unmet, there is going to be hell to pay.

The first question I ask in every premarital counseling session is, "What are your expectations?"

Most of the time they don't even know. So their first assignment is to figure them out, because they will come out. And when they do, watch out.

When I got married, Amy thought I would be Prince Charming, but she found out I was just a horny toad. Ladies, can I get a witness? I thought she would see intimacy as an opportunity, but instead she saw it more as an obligation. What we expected and what we experienced were miles apart. When this happens, disappointment takes root and discouragement takes over.

It sounds a little like this:

If God loved me, this wouldn't have happened.

I hoped our marriage would be better by now, but it's not. Should I move on?

I prayed for that promotion. Why didn't I get it? Is God even listening?

I raised my kids the right way, but they are going the wrong way. Does God even care?

I stayed pure, so why haven't I found the right person yet? Should I just give in?

What you expect and what God wants you to experience are sometimes different. Please do not let what you expect keep you from what God wants you to experience.

Let's read verse thirty-five again, "She conceived again, and when she gave birth to a son she said, 'This time I will praise the Lord.' So she named him Judah. Then she stopped having children."

Notice the phrase, "This time."

For far too long she had been waiting for another person to meet her needs.

If you are constantly waiting for someone else to encourage you, to lift your spirit, to meet all of your needs, it may never happen.

Finally, she stopped waiting for the perfect person to come along and realized she had the power to choose her own happiness.

She said, "This time I will praise the Lord."

Not next time. Not when the perfect time comes.

This time I will praise the Lord.

Sadly, many of us can't get past the last time, while others are waiting for the next time.

We end up living in a state of discouragement because we can't figure out how to be joyful in this time. I hate to break this to you, but you can't change the last time and you don't know if there will be a next time.

So why not praise the Lord this time?

The perfect event or perfect person or perfect time may never come. Stop saying, "When I get that job, when I get that house, when I get that promotion, when my health gets right, when my kids get out of the house, when I get out of debt, then I will praise the Lord."

No you won't. It will be something else.

David wrote, "This is the day the LORD has made. I will rejoice and be glad in it." (Psalm 118:24) NLT

Notice it says, "This is the day."

Not yesterday.

Not tomorrow.

This is the day the Lord has made.

I will rejoice and be glad today, because I don't know if there will be a tomorrow.

Why wait until my marriage gets right, or my kids get right, or my boss gets right, or my health gets right to praise the Lord? It may never happen so rejoice and be glad today. The lies say in order to be happy you need a new spouse, a new job, a bigger house or better health. No. No. No. True joy, the joy I seek, is not determined by what happens to me, but by what Christ is doing in me.

Consider it pure joy, my brothers and sisters, whenever you face trials of many kinds, because you know that the testing of your faith produces perseverance. Let perseverance finish its work so that you may be mature and complete, not lacking anything. (James 1:2-4) NIV

James says that in order to have pure, genuine joy, you might have to go through some stuff. You may not see what God is doing today, but you will someday.

Six Out of Twelve Ain't Too Bad

Jacob's name was eventually changed to Israel. Leah ended up having six boys. That means she gave birth to half of the twelve tribes of Israel. Levi would become the Father of the Priests. From Judah's lineage came the Lion of the Tribe of Judah. From her body, from her burden, came the ultimate blessing. From her suffering came the Savior. From Jacob's mistake came the Messiah. From her son came God's Son!

God has plans for you that you know nothing about right now. That means He might take you through the mess in order to get you to the miracle. It's through our mess God does His best work.

What can we do in this messy time? Praise, rejoice, have joy, because nothing will bring us into the awareness of God's presence more quickly than praising Him in this time. And nothing will take us out of His presence more quickly than by looking to the next time. Her husband didn't love her the way she deserved and that is terrible, but things could have been worse…she could have been barren.

Don't believe me? Ask Hannah.

Married With No Children

Hannah lived during a period in Israel's history known as the Judges. It was the time before Israel had a king. As a result, the people did whatever seemed right in their own eyes, creating a cycle of disobedience, oppression, forgiveness, deliverance, and then disobedience again. The last of the Judges was a man named Samuel. Samuel became one of the greatest prophets in Israel's history, but Samuel almost never made it into the world.

There was a man named Elkanah…Elkanah had two wives, Hannah and Peninnah. Peninnah had children, but Hannah did not. (1 Samuel 1:1-2) NLT

Hannah had a major problem. At this point in her life she was barren. Leah could have kids, but couldn't get love. Hannah could get love, but couldn't have kids. I have said multiple times, I love the Bible. I love it because it is filled with real people with real problems. People who have confidence in who God is, but are conflicted in how He works. It's easy to think the heroes in the Bible were somehow different than we are, but the Bible is filled with real people with real problems who face them with real faith.

In the biblical language, Hannah is barren, but barrenness doesn't begin to describe her pain. For women in the biblical world, infertility was as bad as it gets. Scholars thought it was a sign of disgrace and grounds for divorce. Children were a source of labor for the family and a sign of success for the women who bore them. Not being able to bear children was a sign of present failure and future doom. Barrenness knew no limits as to what oppression might come.

Hannah was not like most women. She knew something most of us don't. She knew God does His best work in our barrenness.

Hannah is one of six women in the Bible described as barren. Sarah, wife of Abraham. Rebekah, wife of Isaac. Rachel, wife of Jacob. Manoah's wife, (we are not given her name). And Elizabeth, wife of Zechariah. Eventually through the power of God, each of these women had a child.

Sarah gave birth to Isaac. Rebekah gave birth to Jacob and Esau. Rachel gave birth to Joseph. Manoah's wife gave birth to Samson. Hannah gave birth to Samuel. Elizabeth gave birth to John the Baptist. From these men came the fathers of the Hebrew nation, the seed of God's promise.

In God's economy, what you start with is not what you are stuck with. Your present limitations may be the very thing God uses to lead you to your future destiny. Too many of us are so stuck looking at what is missing that we can't see what is possible.

Not Hannah.

Her limitation would not keep her from God's limitless supply.

Since Hannah was unable to have children, Elkanah took a second wife, named Peninnah. She was anything but barren. She seemed to have a baby every time he walked into the room. Their house was filled with the sound of children, but none of them were Hannah's. The ache in her heart must have run deep because Peninnah couldn't keep her mouth shut. She found a thousand and one ways to remind Hannah of her inadequacy by flaunting her babies and mocking her barrenness.

Every time Hannah heard a baby cry it must have cut like a knife.

Let's Play House

I'm sure Hannah dreamed of the day a baby would crawl up into her lap and call her mommy.

So many expectations, yet no experiences to go along with them.

For most people, when expectations go unmet, it is easy for anger, resentment, and bitterness to creep in.

Hannah was not like most people.

Year after year this man went up from his town to worship and sacrifice to the Lord Almighty at Shiloh…Whenever the day came for Elkanah to sacrifice, he would give portions of the meat to his wife Peninnah and to all her sons and daughters. But to Hannah he gave a double portion because he loved her, and the Lord had closed her womb. Because the Lord had closed Hannah's womb, her rival kept provoking her in order to irritate her. This went on year after year. Whenever Hannah went up to the house of the Lord, her rival provoked her till she wept and would not eat. (1 Samuel 1:3-7) NIV

Put yourself in this situation. Three times a year the men were required to offer sacrifices at the temple. Three times a year, year after year, she went to worship the Lord, yet every time she went to worship, she was mocked for her worship.

Would you look forward to worship if you knew every time you went you would be mocked? What was she being mocked for? God hasn't answered her prayers.

If we are being honest, most of us would never make it halfway to Shiloh.

Isn't half the battle just showing up?

That's what Hannah did year after year. She kept showing up. Even when she was broken, even when she was unhappy, even when she was defeated, even when she was discouraged, even when she didn't understand, even when God remained silent, even while being mocked…she kept showing up. There is something powerful about a man or woman who keeps showing up when the times are rough, when the days are long, and when God remains silent.

We have a lady in our church who went through nine rounds of fertility treatments. Nine times she was told they didn't work. On the last try, the doctor told her to give up and consider fostering or adopting. She wouldn't give up. She kept praying. Every Saturday she kept showing up to our prayer meeting. What was she praying for? A baby.

February at Mountain View Church is called Miracle Month, a time we come together for prayer and fasting. The last Sunday of the month is called Miracle Sunday. It is a day we give to the Lord a sacrificial offering. On each giving envelope is a space where people can write what miracle they are seeking. We conclude the month by praying over the envelopes and the people who gave them. Kim showed up that Sunday, as she does every Sunday, and when it came time to give her sacrificial offering, she quietly slipped her envelope into the bucket. What did she write on the top of her envelope? For God to bless her barren womb.

Consider God

Elkanah tried his best to comfort Hannah. Even if she never had children he promised he would always love her. He even tried to console her by saying, "You have me—isn't that better than having ten sons?" No sir, it's not!

Despite her barrenness, despite her insecurity, despite her unfulfilled and unmet expectations, she kept showing up. Not only did she keep showing up, she kept sending her prayers up. She prayed until the tears starting flowing, mascara started running, and snot start falling. This woman prayed like she meant it. She prayed earnestly and honestly. She gave God everything she had and waited for Him to do what only He could do.

She decided that instead of dwelling on her unchanging circumstance, she would focus on her unchanging God. Instead of standing in the outer courts, she decided to walk boldly into the presence of God. Deep inside of Hannah, buried beneath years of deferred hopes and dashed dreams was a kernel of faith. A little bit of faith. Just enough to get her to the altar and plead before the only One who could change the situation. She wept loudly and prayed boldly, "God give me a son." She wouldn't let what she was missing keep her from praying for what she wanted.

She made a vow, saying, "Lord Almighty, if you will only look on your servant's misery and remember me, and not forget your servant but give her a son, then I will give him to the Lord for all the days of his life…she kept on praying to the Lord." (vs. 11-12) NIV

The Bible says, "We receive not because we ask not." Sometime you have to ask more than once. Sometimes you have to pray it through before God comes through.

Persistence pays off.

In Luke 18 the persistent widow kept coming to the judge. Luke says that she wore the judge out with her constant request.

When was the last time you wore God out with your constant prayers? When was the last time you took your grief to the Lord and stayed there until He answered? When was the last time you wrestled with God all night and wouldn't let go until He blessed you? When was the last time you knocked on the door of heaven until your knuckles were raw? When was the last time you prayed a gut wrenching, heart pounding prayer that didn't just bend His ear, but touched His heart? When was the last time you prayed until you lost your voice? When was the last time you cried until your tears ran dry?

The sad truth is, most of us would rather run away than pray it away. But those who pray it through, will eventually see God come through. Prayer invites God into the situation, and when God gets involved, all bets are off. Every time God shows up the situation changes. So pray it down until God's presence comes down. You might just be one prayer away from everything changing.

All it takes is for one touch of God's favor to change the trajectory of your life. One good break, one good idea, one new connection, one person who notices you, one answer to your prayers, and all of a sudden everything changes. If you just believe it's possible, God can do in a moment what should have taken a lifetime.

This could be your year to meet the right person. This could be the year your health improves. This could be the year you pay off your debt or beat that addiction. This could be your year for a breakthrough, but breaking through always starts in our thinking. You have to believe it is possible and you have to keep praying until it becomes visible.

Jesus said, "It shall be done according to your faith." Whose faith? Yours. How do you show your faith? You keep showing up. If you keep showing up, God will eventually show up. When that happens, the enemies you once faced will be no more. The habits that held you back will be no more. The doors that were once closed will be opened. The no will turn into yes. The, "not now," will turn into, "now is your time." The limits will be removed and the lid will come off. Your barren womb will be blessed.

Jesus said, "God's Spirit sent me to announce, 'This is God's year to act!'" (Luke 4:18) MSG

Not next year. Not five years. Not in the sweet by and by. This is the year God will shift things in your favor and it will be better than you thought. It will happen quicker than you imagined and it will be more rewarding than you ever dreamed possible. When you honor God, He will honor you. When you are obedient to Him, He will open up the windows of heaven for you. When you keep showing up, I promise you, God will show up.

Hannah believed this.

Happy Hour

Eli, the Priest, observed her prayers. He said to her, "Go in peace! May the God of Israel grant the request you have asked of him." (vs. 17) NIV

She knew God would come through, so she got up and left her doubts at the door.

The next few verses say when they returned home, her husband Elkanah went in and slept with her. God would do His part, but she would have to do hers too.

The LORD remembered her plea, and in due time she gave birth to a son. She named him Samuel, for she said, "I asked the LORD for him." (vs. 19b-20) NLT

In the Hebrew Samuel means, "God has heard." Every time she said his name she was reminded that if you keep showing up, God will eventually show up!

The Lord was gracious to Hannah; she gave birth to three sons and two daughters. Meanwhile, the boy Samuel grew up in the presence of the Lord. (1 Samuel 2:21) NIV

When you make worshiping God your goal, and give back to Him what He gave to you, you will always receive back a greater portion. God gave her back more than she asked for, three sons and two daughters to be exact. Samuel went on to become one of the most influential leaders in Israel's history, arguably the greatest biblical character between Moses and David. Hannah's faithfulness didn't just impact her life, it affected an entire nation!

I Heard a Cry

During the last ten days of our Miracle Month we meet together every morning for prayer. This past February, during our individual time of prayer, I heard a few sounds coming from the back of the room. It sounded like a baby.

I didn't think much about it because parents often bring their children with them. As the individual part of our prayer time concluded and we came together to pray as a group, I noticed Kim was holding a baby. As we formed our circle, Kim spoke up. She said, "Pastor, one year ago today, I prayed for this baby one last time before exploring other options. The moment I gave my sacrificial gift, doubt left my mind. I knew God would be faithful and here is my beautiful, healthy baby girl to prove it."

The longer I am in ministry, the less I am impressed with people who start something. What impresses me now is the faith it takes to keep showing up, even when it seems like God isn't.

Sermon in a sentence: If you keep showing up, God will eventually show up.

MIGHTY WARRIOR BUT STILL WORRIED

CHAPTER 6
THE STORY OF GIDEON

Have you ever been given a label? The smart kid, funny kid, rich kid, poor kid, cute kid, or athletic kid? How about single, broke, divorced, widowed, bankrupt, or temperamental? Maybe even a felon, a drop out, an alcoholic, or junkie?

The strange thing about labels is they have a tendency to stick your entire life. Think about it. When you go to a class reunion or come across a former classmate, how do you describe them?

Everyone Looks Old…Except Me

A few years ago, my father-in-law had his fortieth class reunion. The first thing he said when he got back was that everyone looked old. For the next several minutes he described his former classmates. I saw Jim. Jim was the football player. There was Tina. She was a nerd so I didn't know her very well. I ran across Mike. Almost didn't recognize him. Mike was the drummer in the band. I even saw Steve. Never thought Steve would make it because he was a stoner. Stephanie sure looked different too. She used to be the hot cheerleader. You know you are getting old when the hot girl in school just had a hip replacement.

It was funny listening to him describe his former classmates and I could tell that in his mind, he still looked and felt eighteen.

Don't we all?

The thing that stuck with me though, was that forty years later he is still identifying people by the labels given to them in high school.

Anyone Seen the Label Maker?

Everyone has labels, but let's be fair, we have also labeled other people.

They aren't always dramatic. Most people nowadays refer to me as Pastor Daniel. It doesn't matter where I go, Pastor is almost always their first description of me. I think they are warning people ahead of time to watch what they say.

I am also a husband, a dad, a brother, and a son.

Depending on where I am and who I am with determines the label I have in that moment.

Labeling is nothing new. People throughout history have been remembered by their labels, such as Alexander the Great, Billy the Kid, Andre the Giant and Jabba the Hutt.

We even remember people in the Bible by their labels. Some are labeled by the circumstances surrounding their birth while others are labeled by a physical characteristic at birth. Remember Jacob the hustler and Esau the hairy monster? Some are labeled by their heroics. Moses was the deliverer and Benaiah was the lion chaser. Some are labeled by their deeds, whether good or bad. Thomas was a doubter, Rahab was a prostitute, and Judas was the betrayer. Some are labeled by their job like Matthew the tax collector. Simon was even labeled by his passion, Simon the zealot. Another Simon was labeled by Jesus as Peter the rock. Paul was labeled by his calling, the apostle to the Gentiles.

Some labels we have even given ourselves. I'm damaged. I'm a drunk. I'm an addict. I'm fat. I'm ugly. I'm washed up. I'm stupid. I'm a failure. Some labels doctors have given to us. I'm ADD, LD, or ADHD. I'm handicapped. I'm bipolar. Some counselors have placed them upon us. I'm mentally unstable, a manic, clinical, or codependent.

Most labels are innocent, but others hurt deeply. I am almost forty years old, but some of the labels given to me I will never forget.

When I was in the third grade I wrestled in a national tournament. I was doing really well and found myself in the semifinals. The tournament took place in the middle of January at the Tulsa Fairgrounds Arena. The arena has twenty-four sets of doors and to get from the stands to the arena floor you have to walk through the hallways past the doors. With as many people coming and going as there normally are in a tournament this size, the hallways were extremely cold. Will Rogers once said about Oklahoma, "If you don't like the weather, stay a day, because it will change by tomorrow."

By late afternoon, a severe winter storm had blown in, making it unreasonably cold. The only thing I had to wear was a wrestling singlet and t-shirt. All day long I walked back and forth from the wrestling mat to the stands, which meant I went from being extremely sweaty to having cold chills. As you can imagine, it didn't take long for me to get sick, and by evening I was running a high temperature. My semifinal match was one of the last matches of the night. Long story short, I ended up losing the match. It was a match I should have won and I will never forget what my dad said to me after the match, "Daniel, you're a quitter. You're weak. A loser." I was eight years old but I can still hear those words today.

The second label given to me was in the eighth grade. I moved from a large urban school to a smaller rural one. I will never forget walking into the lunch room for the first time and hearing someone say, "He is not one of us. He's an outsider." And that is exactly how they treated me.

The third label came when I was in high school. My dad really wanted me to get a college scholarship in baseball. One day I overheard my dad and coach discussing what opportunities I may have after graduating. The coach said to my dad, "Randy, he's good, but he's not that good. He's a slightly above average ball player."

Do you mind if I give you one more?

My fourth label came when I was pastoring my first church. There were two men in the church whom I swear made it their personal goal to make my life miserable and I have to hand it to them, they accomplished their goal. Fifteen years later I still refer to these men as Sanballat and Tobiah. (If you have no idea why, read the book of Nehemiah.) What was most hurtful is I had known these two men my entire life. One of them used to babysit me as a child and he and his wife were very influential in the early years of my parents' marriage. He loved me as the Youth Pastor, but the moment I became Lead Pastor, it was game on. I did everything I could to pacify these two men, but no matter what I did, they would ridicule it, mock it, and vote against it. I had never been treated as badly as I was by those two leaders in our church.

One Sunday evening, just before the service began, I was entering the sanctuary when one of our church employees approached me. He said, "You won't believe what so and so just said about you." I said, "Trust me, I know what he is saying about me." He decided to tell me anyway. "I heard him say you are destroying the church by making bad decisions." He then said, "He is not worth the money the church is paying him."

There you have it. I have been labeled a quitter, weak, an outsider, average, not good enough, and not worth the Lord's money.

Of course, I have been given many positive labels as well. In the seventh grade I was voted Mr. Legs. Top that suckers! I have also been Homecoming King, Class President, and Salutatorian. But what labels do you think I hear in my mind over and over again? I don't have to tell you.

Those labels not only hurt then, but they still hurt today. They go through my mind every time I stand to speak, start to write, or begin to lead.

In fact, as I am writing right now these are the thoughts running through my mind:

"No one is going to buy this book. You're not interesting or smart enough to write a book. You're too simple, not deep enough. You have nothing to say that hasn't been said before. You're just a country boy. Why would anyone care about you? Seriously, why would anyone buy this book? Next time you're in Goodwill you're gonna find this book in the bargain bin. Better have this book spell checked and fact checked a hundred times because you know you're gonna screw something up. Go ahead and quit now, you're just wasting your time. You're a sorry writer, terrible story teller, and nobody likes you."

All of that went through my mind in the last thirty seconds. If you could hear the conversations I have in my head while I'm preaching, you would have me institutionalized.

Am I messed up? Probably.

But I don't think I am the only one who hears voices in their head like this.

Our situations may be different, but our struggles are the same.

We are conflicted.

I am not trying to get you to feel sorry for me. I am past that. Well, I'm working on it.

What I am trying to get you to see is, labels are powerful. Labels lock us into old patterns and lock new opportunities out. At any moment you have two voices speaking to you. One comes to lock you into the patterns of your past and to rob you of the future God has in store. The other comes to give life. Not just any life, but a full, abundant, overflowing, joyful life.

There are many things you don't have control over. You didn't choose when, where, or to whom you'd be born. God, in His sovereignty, chose those things. But there is one thing you do have control over and it may be the most important thing: You choose what you believe about yourself. You can believe what God says about you, or you can believe what others say about you. It's your choice. Whichever voice you choose to believe will determine the life that you live.

One of the greatest gifts God gives His children is the power of choice. I may not be able to control what happens to me, but I can control how I view what happens to me.

It's No Wonder

I read recently that most Americans have around 60,000 thoughts a day with over 80% of them being negative. In other words, from the moment we get up in the morning to the moment we lie down at night, our mind is consumed with negativity. Most of them are centered around the idea of not being enough. Not slim enough, not pretty enough, not smart enough, not good enough.

Go ahead and fill in the blank. I am not ___________ enough.

Those are the predominant thoughts running through our minds every day.

The problem is, the thoughts you consume end up consuming you.

And whatever consumes your mind controls you.

So what are you letting consume your mind? What's causing you to feel so insecure that you can't see any hope when you look in the mirror? What worry is eating away at you so that you can't sleep at night? What fear is crippling you so you can't see any light at the end of the tunnel? What voice have you heard that is still whispering to you, "You are not good enough, smart enough, or strong enough?" What voice is saying that nothing is going to change?

If you don't control these thoughts they will control you, cripple you, and lock you into a self-defeating pattern while locking out any new opportunity God has for you.

The Apostle Paul strongly encourages us to take every thought captive in 2 Corinthians 10:5. It is impossible to control everything that flies around in our mind, but we can control what we allow to land. I choose what I focus on. I can focus on what others say about me or what God says about me.

What I focus on I end up feeling, so it might do us some good if we spent more time thinking about what we are thinking about.

Barney Fife to Marshall Dillion

Have you ever heard of Gideon? No, he is not the guy who puts the Bible in the hotel drawers. Gideon was a judge. Judges were civil leaders and authorities in Israel. It was their job to administer justice and lead the people against opposition. God was in charge, but the judge carried out His will. Sadly, during the time known as the Judges, Israel kept doing what was right in their own eyes.

Gideon's story begins with us being introduced to the Midianites. The Midianites were cruel people. Every harvest season they would sweep in and steal the crops from the Israelites. If a new animal was born, they would take it too. They took almost everything the Israelites had. This went on for seven years. The strange thing about the Midianites is they weren't numerous enough to wage war by themselves, so they would often create coalitions with surrounding nations to reap havoc on the people of God. As a result, most of the Israelites were living in caves up in the mountains, starving to death.

Apparently they'd had enough and began to cry out to God for help.

He replied by saying, "I brought you out of slavery from Egypt. I have already driven the enemies from the land once. I even gave you their land, but you won't listen to me, so you're getting what you deserve!"

Do you ever get tired of reading about how dumb the Israelites were? I do. Sometimes I want to say, "Stick it to them God. Give them what they deserve!" Then I remember how dumb I am and thank God for being so gracious to me.

Worry Wart

The angel of the LORD came and sat beneath the great tree at Ophrah, which belonged to Joash of the clan of Abiezer. Gideon, son of Joash, was threshing wheat at the bottom of a winepress to hide the grain from the Midianites. (Judges 6:11) NLT

This is our first mention of Gideon. He is hiding at the bottom of a winepress trying to get a little wheat to feed his family.

The first words the angel of the Lord says to him are, "The LORD is with you, mighty warrior!" (vs. 12) NIV

Mighty warrior? He's hiding in a winepress. He seems more like a worrier than a warrior.

Did you know that currently 40 million Americans over the age of eighteen are suffering from chronic anxiety and worry? Anxiety and emotional disorders have increased 44% the past five years. One in six Americans are currently on some sort of prescription drug to deal with their anxiety. The group most affected is the thirty to forty age range, with the under eighteen crowd not far behind.

What about you? Are you a worrier? Symptoms of worry include: loss of sleep, muscle tension, not able to stay calm or sit still, indigestion, paranoia, shortness of breath, heart palpitations, cold hands, and dry mouth. Synonyms for worry are: concerned, uneasy, apprehensive, fearful, troubled, bothered, disturbed, distressed, agitated, nervous, edgy, antsy, tense, worked up, jumpy, and stomach in knots.

If you weren't worried a few moments ago I bet you are now!

Seriously, have you experienced anxiety in the last week? I know I have. As I've already told you, just writing this makes me worrisome.

We live in the age of worry. Worry is as American as apple pie and is a sign of the times we live in. It is even marketed to us by the people who feed us our information. Think about it. Advertisers engage us by using fear tactics and they use these fear tactics to create anxiety so they can promote drug companies to help keep us calm. The problem is, these agencies are often owned by the same companies. They scare us, then sell to us. Twisted, isn't it?

When Paul writes in Philippians 4:6 to be anxious for nothing, we say, "Yeah right, Paul! You may be in prison, but you are not in America."

But dealing with worry seems to be an overwhelming theme in Scripture. Even the rock Peter wrote in his later years, "Cast all your anxiety on him…" (1 Peter 5:7) NIV

Apparently, even the strongest of men have a tendency to worry. Such is the case for Gideon.

Listen to his reply.

"Sir," Gideon replied, "If the LORD is with us, why has all this happened to us? And where are all the miracles our ancestors told us about? Didn't they say, 'The LORD brought us up out of Egypt?' But now the LORD has abandoned us and handed us over to the Midianites." (vs. 13) NLT

His reply is filled with doubt, fear, anger, anxiety, and resentment. "If God is so good, why is all this bad stuff happening to us?" Typical question, isn't it?

I have discovered in life there are two types of suffering: the unexplainable and explainable. Sometimes things happen with no logical explanation, making it unexplainable. However, most of the tragedies that happen in life are explainable. It is simply cause and effect. If you smoke, chances are high you will get cancer. If you drink and drive, chances are high you will get in a wreck. If you do drugs, chances are high your body is going to break down. If you treat your spouse like dirt, chances are high they will leave you. If you neglect your kids, chances are high they will exhibit anger toward you. If you eat poorly, chances are high you will be overweight and have a variety of health challenges. If you are a bad employee, chances are high you will get fired. If you are thirty-five and live in your parent's basement, chances are high you will never get married.

Most of the suffering in the world falls into the explainable category.

At least that is true for my life. Most of my suffering is self-inflicted.

The same was true for the Israelites.

That is why God doesn't even answer the question, because Gideon knows why this is happening.

The LORD turned to him and said, "Go in the strength you have, and rescue Israel from the Midianites. I am sending you!" "But Lord," Gideon replied, "how can I rescue Israel? My clan is the weakest in the whole tribe of Manasseh, and I am the least in my entire family!" (vs. 14-15) NLT

Someone, at some point in time, had labeled Gideon and his family. Someone had told them they weren't important, they didn't matter, and they were the weakest of Manasseh's tribes. They were also told they were no good and couldn't be used, so at some point in their family history, they started to believe it. They started to believe this might just be who they are, and there may not be anything they could do about it.

Labels had locked Gideon and his family in and locked God out.

Gideon said, "We are Ophrahites."

Ophrah means the place of dust.

In other words, we are nothing but a nuisance to people and if they could wipe us off the map they would.

Not only is his clan the weakest, but he also believes he is the runt of the family.

God you've got the wrong village, the wrong family, and the wrong kid.

All of us have been on the outside looking in. Nothing feels worse than being told you don't belong because we all have a longing for belonging. Whether it be in the lunch room or the board room, we all want to know we have a place at the table.

Please Back Away From the Label Maker

Who has the right to label you?

Can I come into your home and start labeling whatever I want? No.

There are only two people who have the right to label something: The one who made it and the one who purchased it.

I can come into your home and label something, and I may even be right, but I don't have the right, because I didn't create it nor do I own it.

Let this sink deep into your soul: God is the only one who has the right to label you because He is the only one who created you and purchased you.

You made all the delicate, inner parts of my body and knit me together in my mother's womb. Thank you for making me so wonderfully complex! Your workmanship is marvelous—how well I know it. (Psalm 139:13-14) NLT

When was the last time you believed that if God said you are wonderful, then you must be wonderful? When was the last time you gave yourself permission to believe you had what it takes? When was the last time you believed that you are favored, you are gifted, you are a masterpiece, you are valued, you are wonderful, and you are loved? When was the last time you looked into the mirror and declared, "I am marvelous!"

The Bible says that about you. You do believe the Bible, don't you?

I think too many of us are insulting our Creator by insulting His work. When we believe the worst about ourselves we are telling God He didn't do a good enough job putting us together. We would never say it, but we think it, "God, if I were You I would have done this differently. I would have made me skinnier, taller, and smarter. I would have given me a better spouse, better parents, better kids, and a better education. I would have given me more talents and less appetite."

God could have solved every one of your problems as your Creator. So maybe your problem isn't with others, maybe it's with God.

Changes things, doesn't it?

I don't know too many people who would admit they have a problem with God, so if we have a problem saying it, maybe we shouldn't think it.

When we accept the label someone else gives us, we are ignoring the one God has given us, and in doing that we are insulting our Maker.

This is what Gideon is doing. He is telling God, "I don't have everything I need to do all that You are calling me to do. I feel deficient."

In other words, I think You are holding back from me. If You really loved me then You would give me more.

The Lord answered Gideon's worry by saying, "Go in the strength you have," and, "I will be with you." (vs. 14, 16)

I have given you everything you need to do everything I am asking you to do and I will be with you through it all.

What more could you need?

God is saying, "Gideon, it is not about what you can do, it's about what I can do through you."

If God left it out of your life, then you don't need it in your life.

Stop worrying about what you don't have and start looking at what you do have.

In Exodus 4:2 The Lord asked Moses, "What's in your hand?"

It was a simple shepherd's staff, a symbol of his identity, income and influence.

God was asking Moses to give back what He had given to him.

Here's an interesting fact. Every time Moses laid the staff down, the staff came to life and every time he took it back up, it died.

Maybe we should lay more things down and stop holding on to them so tightly.

What's In Your Hand?

God has entrusted each of us with unique talents, abilities and gifts. They may not seem like much. They may just be a staff like Moses or a slingshot like David or a simple sack lunch like the little boy with five fish and two loaves. But whatever it is, God has given it to you to accomplish the purpose He has for you.

So what's in your hand?

What do you already have at your disposal that you may be overlooking because you think it is small or insignificant?

Whatever it is, it is enough.

If you want to get over your fear of not having enough or being enough, start by taking a good inventory of what you already have.

Gratitude kills greed but it also fuels contentment. Being content is being confident that what we have is enough.

If you needed a better family, God would have given it. If you need more money, He will provide it. If you need more education, He will allow it. If you need a better job or bigger house, you'll get it. If not, you don't need it.

Peter wrote, "By his divine power, God has given us everything we need for living a godly life." (2 Peter 1:3) NLT

The psalmist echoes this in Psalm 139. He took a good inventory of what he has by saying, "What I have is enough." That is why he says in verse 14, "I know your works full well."

In other words, every time I get up in the morning and look around or look at myself, I see I am blessed. I am fearfully and wonderfully made. If I am a little heavier than I desire at the moment, I don't complain. I just say to myself, "It may not be what my wife wants, but that's okay, because it's gonna be more than she wants! It's more for her to love. So thank you Lord for giving me all of this!"

At the end of the chapter David says, "Search me, O God and know my heart; test me and know my anxious thoughts." (Psalm 139:23) NIV

In other words, I have searched myself, and now I need You to search me too. Please reveal to me anything that might make me anxious.

Those two words, "search me," would set us free from 90% of our anxieties because so much of our anxiety is caused by worrying about other people and situations beyond our control. David knows nothing will ever change until he changes his way of thinking.

It is not what happens externally that makes me anxious, but what I allow to reside in my mind.

There is a difference between feeling anxiety and being anxious. There will be always moments when our hands shake or palms get sweaty. That's normal. What is abnormal is when things are going well but we cannot enjoy it because we are anticipating a shoe to drop.

It's not a person or a problem or even a physical pain that causes worry. It is a thinking process.

So David makes a hard turn from the external enemies he can't control to the one internal enemy he can control, his thought life.

He learned the hard way that only one person's opinion matters. It isn't mom or dad, husband or wife, boss or best friend. The only one whose opinion matters is the One who created you and purchased you.

You were bought at a price… (1 Corinthians 6:20) NIV

He has purchased us to be His own people… (Ephesians 1:14) NLT

If you have trusted in Jesus as your Savior, you have been purchased by His blood. Therefore, He is the only one with the right to label you.

Let me give you permission to shed the labels others have placed on you and accept the one God has given you.

I want you to say to yourself right now, "I am anointed. I am blessed. I am a child of the King. I am chosen. I am a citizen of heaven. I am more than a conqueror. I am empowered. I am enough. I am favored. I am forgiven. I am free. I am His friend. I am loved. I am God's masterpiece. I am God's messenger. I am an overcomer. I am a saint. I am the light of the world. I am the salt of the earth. I am a mighty warrior."

Gideon, it doesn't matter what others say about you. What matters is what I say about you. "You are a mighty warrior." Stop believing you are nothing. Stop believing you are insignificant. Stop believing you an outsider and start believing you are a mighty hero.

Every time you believe the labels other people have placed on you something inside of you dies. Some of you have let God's vision for your life, or your marriage, or your kids, or maybe even His vision for your future, die. Some of you have lost your vision to start a new company, to start a new career, or to go back to school.

It's time you resurrect those dead dreams!

How? By taking every thought captive and making it obedient to Christ.

You have to think about what you are thinking about.

If you know who you are and Whose you are, you can overcome any obstacle. It doesn't matter if it is a pink slip, a bad diagnosis, a termination notice, or a divorce certificate. You can overcome it.

It's time to let the enemy know he has no right to label you because he didn't create you nor did he purchase you.

Overpower the lies of the enemy with the promises of God.

Thoughts are the seeds to actions, so if you really want to change your life, you have to change the way you think about yourself. Give yourself permission to believe you have what it takes.

A New Way to Fight

The story goes on to say Gideon defeated an army of 135,000 Midianites with 300 men. How did he defeat them? With what he already had in his hands, trumpets and clay jars.

If God is inside you and grace has transformed you, then you are a force to be reckoned with.

It is time you start living like a victorious child of God.

I beg you to stop living in defeat. Don't count yourself out just yet because your struggle may be the starting place for God's victory in your life. You were not created to live an average, ordinary, unrewarding, unfulfilled life. God created you to leave a mark on this generation and break barriers for the kingdom.

But the break out starts in our thinking.

Let God transform you into a new person by changing the way you think. (Romans 12:2) NLT

If you want to become a new person then start thinking in a new way. I know it has been a long journey and you haven't seen much change, but this is a new day. New seeds have been sown, so let them take root. Let them give you a renewed sense of expectancy. Anticipation and expectation are the breeding grounds for miracles to take place. So live with a sense of expectancy because God wants to do greater things than you can imagine. Things so great that only He can receive the glory. Things so awesome and powerful that when people look at your life, the sole response they can come up with is, "Only God."

That's what happens when 300 men armed with clay pots and lanterns take down an army of 135,000!

Who Opened the Flood Gates?

In 1 Chronicles 14 David and his men were up against the mighty Philistines. They were greatly outnumbered and had little chance of winning. David asked God for help and God promised to go with him to defeat the opposing army.

So David and his troops went up to Baal-perazim and defeated the Philistines there. "God did it!" David exclaimed. "He used me to burst through my enemies like a raging flood!" So they named that place Baal-perazim (which means "the Lord who bursts through"). (1 Chronicles 14:11) NLT

I love how David describes God's power. He says it comes in like a raging flood. When the God of the breakthrough shows up and releases His power, nothing can stop it.

I don't care how difficult the obstacles may seem or how unattainable your dream may be, when God releases a flood of His goodness, a flood of His favor, and a flood of His healing upon your life, nothing can stop it. The sickness may look big, but when He releases His healing it doesn't stand a chance. Your opposition may be better equipped, but when God releases His floodgates even your enemies will be at peace with you. You may not have the friends or the funding, but you don't need them when you have God's favor.

LORD, you bless the righteous; you surround them with your favor… (Psalm 5:12) BSB

If You Only Just Believe

There are two voices speaking to you right now. One is a voice of suspicion. It may even be whispering that this is all religious hyperbole, positive rhetoric or poisonous optimism, yet there is another voice inside of you that wants to believe this so badly.

Whichever voice you feed, grows. Whichever one you starve, dies.

Why not feed the voice of faith today? You've fed the voice of doubt and insecurity for too long. It's time to raise your expectations, shake off your self-pity, get rid of your negativity, delete your disappointments, eliminate your fears, repent of your sinfulness and say, "God, I'm ready for a breakthrough! I am making room for a flood of Your favor!"

Christians are not supposed to drag through life defeated. As a Christian, you have the label of favor. So speak that over your frustrations. Speak that over your fears. Speak that over your failures. Speak that over your labels.

Let me repeat, as a child of God you have been given favor. When you believe you have favor, you realize you have the advantage. So put those shoulders back and hold that head high. Don't be discouraged by your situation. You have what it takes because you have the favor of God.

Nehemiah stood before the king and his enemies and said, "There is something about me you can't see, something that can't be put on paper. It's called favor."

The city tried to shut him down and the critics tried to stop him, but he accomplished in fifty-two days what should have taken a year.

When you know God's favor is upon you, you will accomplish your dreams faster than you ever thought possible.

Declare today, just like Nehemiah did:

I have God's favor upon me!

Call me Mr. or Mrs. Baskin-Robbins because I have thirty-one flavors of God's favor!

It's time we quit thinking negative, self-defeating thoughts, and start thanking God for what He has placed in our hands. You don't need to come from fame when you have favor. You don't need to come from fortune when you have favor. God's favor will take you where you cannot go on your own and put you in front of people you never thought you would meet.

Pray this with me.

"Father, thank You for Your favor. Others may not see it, but I know the truth. No matter who or what comes against me. No matter what others say or don't say about me, I will not worry anymore. You said I am a mighty warrior, so today I am going to start believing it. You have already placed in my hands what I need to overcome the enemy and achieve the victory. In Jesus I have everything I need. Amen."

David said, "When darkness overtakes the righteous, light comes bursting in!" (Psalm 112:4) TLB

Not trickling in, but bursting in.

If you prayed that prayer and believe it as much as you are able to at this moment, even though it may be dark right now, I promise you, God's favor is about to come bursting in.

Sermon in a Sentence: The label you accept will determine the life you experience.

CHAPTER 7
THE STORY OF SAUL

No matter where we've come from, or how many accolades we've received, we want a place to belong. If I am being honest, most days I feel I don't belong on a stage. Others are more qualified than I am. Others have better vernacular and grammatical skills. Others are more educated and more eloquent. Others are more deserving and better suited to lead the church.

This may surprise you, but I pray almost every week, "Lord, if you have someone better to pastor this church I will gladly move out of the way." I am terrified I am going to mess up what God is doing. In the most authentic way possible, I know myself, and when I look in the mirror I have to admit I am flawed. I assume many of you have felt that way a time or two as well. On certain days and in certain environments we feel we are not qualified to live the life we are living or do the things we are doing. No matter how many successes have come our way, or how many people like our posts on social media, we are keenly aware of our sins and shortcomings. We don't need anyone to tell us how bad we are because we already know it. When I look in the mirror I can come up with many excuses as to why I couldn't, or shouldn't, be the one God uses.

You and I are not the only ones who feel this way. Gideon felt this way, Moses felt this way, Isaiah felt this way, Jeremiah felt this way, and Esther felt this way. They all went kicking and screaming into their calling. The problem is, you and I have a tendency to hide behind these excuses. Those logical, legitimate reasons as to why we are not the one who can get it done.

Have you ever considered that maybe our imperfections are not keeping us from our destiny as much as they are positioning us for it? When God uses us in spite of us, He is the one who receives the glory. I know you have heard the cliché, "God doesn't call the qualified, He qualifies the called." Yes, it is catchy, corny and cute, but it is also true. So listen up! If you feel unqualified, you're not alone. In fact, you are in really good company. Every person in the Bible God chose to use in a meaningful way started with what looked like a meaningless life; no exceptions, not one. They all had a justifiable excuse as to why he or she couldn't, or shouldn't, be used by God to accomplish greater things.

Abraham was old. Jacob was a liar. Leah was ugly. Joseph was misused and abused. Moses had a speaking problem. Gideon was afraid. Samson was a womanizer. Rahab was a prostitute. Jeremiah and Timothy were too young. Sarah was too old. David was an adulterer and a murderer. Elijah was suicidal. Isaiah preached naked. Jonah ran from God. Naomi was a widow. Job was bankrupt. John the Baptist was eccentric. Peter denied Christ. James and John were self-absorbed. Martha worried. Lazarus was dead. The Samaritan woman was divorced multiple times over.

Zacchaeus was a wee little man and money hungry. The Disciples abandoned Jesus. Paul killed Christians.

In the words of Rocky Balboa to the infamous Clubber Lang, "You ain't so bad are you?"

If you have ever had a dream to do something more, to make a difference, to change your family or your community or even your world, but struggled to believe you can, this chapter is for you.

I believe you can.

More importantly God says you can.

Permission granted to believe God can use you and actually wants to use you.

This isn't a matter of believing in yourself. It is a matter of believing in God's ability to use ordinary people to do extraordinary things.

It's called, "Godfidence." A belief in God's desire to work through you.

If this statement is true, just think of its implications and imagine the possibilities. Imagine the problems we could solve, the people we could help, and the pain that could be taken away if we actually believed we are the ones God wants to use.

I heard a pastor say, "The wrong stuff with the right anointing always equals the right person for the job."

Great Priest, Terrible Parent

A few chapters ago we talked about Hannah. After a long period of barrenness God blessed her with a son named Samuel. Samuel became a great man of God who served his nation well. The Bible says he was so in tune with God's voice that He didn't let one of Samuel's words fall to the ground without coming to pass. Wow! Talk about being in step with the Spirit!

However, even though Samuel served his nation well, he apparently did not serve his home well. Sadly, this happens too often in a pastor's home. God's house gets more attention than our own.

As Samuel grew old, he appointed his sons to be judges over Israel. Joel and Abijah, his oldest sons, held court in Beersheba. But they were not like their father, for they were greedy for money. They accepted bribes and perverted justice. Finally, all the elders of Israel met at Ramah to discuss the matter with Samuel. "Look," they told him, "you are now old, and your sons are not like you. Give us a king to judge us like all the other nations have." (1 Samuel 8:1-5) NIV

Did they have a king? Yes.

Who was it? God.

Does it get any better than that? No.

Wouldn't you like to have God as our president? Me too. Me too. Me too!

It was good enough for Israel too, until they started looking around. Every time you start looking at what others have you lose sight of what God has already given you. Every time.

I Wanna Be Cool, Too

No matter who we are, we all want be like the cool kids. They have a king, we need a king. They got a boat, we need a boat. She got a new car, I need a new car. She got her hair cut, I need my hair cut. We are fine with what we have until we start looking at what others have, then all of a sudden we have needs we didn't even know were there. She remodeled her kitchen, mine looks outdated. She got a new dress, mine looks out of style. You didn't even know you weren't mother of the year until you started checking out Pinterest. Before you know it, comparison gets the best of you; her house is nicer than yours, her car is fancier than yours, her selfie in Hawaii is better than yours in Mexico. You were happy until you started checking out what everyone else was doing on social media and now your life stinks.

It's a sick fact of life. The more we look at other people's lives, the less satisfied we are with our own.

No matter how old you are, if someone gets a king, it won't take long until you want one too.

Was what Israel had better? Yes, it was. But, they didn't want what was better; they wanted what everyone else had.

Starter Jacket Syndrome

Do you remember Starter jackets? Those things were all the rage back in the late 80's and early 90's, even in small town Oklahoma. I begged and pleaded with my parents to buy me one. I promised to mow the lawn, do the dishes, and clean the house for a year if they would just buy me one, but they wouldn't.

What did you do when you were a kid and your parents said no to something you wanted? I know what I did. I went to my granny and papa. It didn't take much to convince my granny to buy me a new jacket. Notice I said jacket and not "Starter" jacket. There is a big difference between the two, especially when you are in junior high. My granny bought me a better jacket, but I did not want a better jacket, I wanted a Starter jacket. Quality doesn't matter in junior high. Brand trumps better all day, every day.

When we start comparing our life with other people's, we are forced to wrestle with the same question Israel did. Who or what do I want to be on the throne of my life? Who or what will be in charge?

Samuel was displeased with their request and went to the LORD for guidance. "Do everything they say to you," the LORD replied, "for it is me they are rejecting, not you. They don't want me to be their king any longer. Ever since I brought them from Egypt they have continually abandoned me and followed other gods. And now they are giving you the same treatment. Do as they ask, but solemnly warn them about the way a king will reign over them." (1 Samuel 8:6-8) NLT

So Samuel passed on the LORD's warning to the people who were asking him for a king. "This is how a king will reign over you…" (vs. 10-11) NLT

Samuel then paints a very bleak picture of what being under a king will look like. He ends the section by saying, "You will be his slaves. You will beg for relief from this king you are demanding, but then the LORD will not help you." (vs. 17-18) NLT

It didn't matter. If everyone else had a king, Israel wanted one too.

But the people refused to listen to Samuel's warning. "Even so, we still want a king," they said. "We want to be like the nations around us…" So Samuel repeated to the LORD what the people had said, and the LORD replied, "Do as they say, and give them a king." Then Samuel agreed and sent the people home. (vs. 19-22) NLT

Please read the next line slowly. What we think is best for us may not be what God wants for us.

Let me say it another way. What you think is best for you may not be God's best for you.

You might want to read that again.

Country Music Theology

Do you remember Garth Brooks? I sure hope you do. He's the second greatest country music singer of all time. Who's number one? King George, of course!

Garth had a song called *Unanswered Prayers.*

Here are the lyrics:

Just the other night, at a hometown football game

My wife and I ran into my old high school flame

And as I introduced them, the past came back to me

And I couldn't help but think of the way things used to be

She was the one that I'd wanted for all times

And each night I'd spend prayin' that God would make her mine

And if he'd only grant me this wish I wished back then

I'd never ask for anything again

Sometimes I thank God for unanswered prayers

Remember when you're talkin' to the man upstairs

And just because he doesn't answer doesn't mean he don't care

Some of God's greatest gifts are unanswered prayers

She wasn't quite the angel that I remembered in my dreams

And I could tell that time had changed me,

In her eyes too it seemed

We tried to talk about the old days,

There wasn't much we could recall

I guess the Lord knows what he's doin', after all

And as she walked away, well, I looked at my wife

And then and there I thanked the good Lord,

For the gifts in my life

Sometimes I thank God for unanswered prayers

Remember when you're talkin' to the man upstairs

And just because he may not answer doesn't mean he don't care

Some of God's greatest gifts are unanswered…

Some of God's greatest gifts, are all too often unanswered…

Some of God's greatest gifts are unanswered prayers

Have you ever wanted something so bad you were willing to bargain with God to get it? I have.

Before I met my wife, I met a girl from Louisiana. I had never met a girl from the deep South before and I was love struck. She had dark skin and dark brown hair, a sweet southern accent, and a big contagious cajun smile. She even had all of her teeth, which I heard was a big accomplishment for a girl from the bayou.

I remember begging for God to make her mine. Now here's the thing, I was fourteen and knew her for one week. Still, it was enough.

Summer loving had me a blast

Summer loving happened so fast

For a while we wrote letters back and forth. A few times we even talked on the phone. (Anyone remember *Callin' Baton Rouge* from Garth?) Understand, this was before cell phones and long distance phone calls were too expensive. I liked her, but not that much. (I was saving for a real Starter jacket people! Priorities.) As you can imagine, after a few months I forgot all about her.

During my freshmen year of college I took an Intro to Computers class. In the class we were introduced to this new thing called the Internet. At first, I thought, "This is the dumbest thing ever." Sounds crazy now, doesn't it?

The professor was trying to convince us this was the wave of the future, so he had us type in any person we could think of that we hadn't seen in a while. The first person who came to mind was the Cajun cutie. Sure enough, her name got a hit on the search engine. He told us to click on the link and see where it took us. I don't really know how to describe what happened next other than shock. I don't want to sound mean, but had I married her it would have been like marrying Leah instead of Rachel. She didn't look anything like the way I remembered her. In fact, I almost didn't even recognize her. (If you are reading this and you just so happen to be the girl I am speaking of, I'm so sorry. For the record, you did teach me a very important lesson about life. Some of God's greatest gifts are unanswered prayers. I hope this helps.) The moment I saw her face, the only thing I could do was start singing:

Then and there I thanked the good Lord

For the gifts in my life

Just because he may not answer doesn't mean he don't care

Some of God's greatest gifts are unanswered prayers

Oh great theologian Garth Brooks, you are so right.

Let me say it again, what you think is best for you may not be God's best for you!

Seriously, aren't you glad God hasn't answered all of your prayers the way you wanted Him to? If you think back over your life I bet you prayed for some things you're glad you didn't get. I certainly am because what God gave me was far better. God gave me a country cutie with a rock-'n'-roll booty! Yes, I just said that. Mama always told me if you think something good you should say it. I figure writing it is better. Miss Amy is an answer to a prayer I wasn't smart enough to pray.

Craig Groeschel says, "If God met all of your expectations He would not be able to exceed them." He sure exceeded mine. When God made Amy, He was just showing off. She is my Ephesians 3:20 and because she is more than enough, I can't get enough! Take that devil. Trying to get me to settle for a Golden Corral steak when God had a Ruth's Chris waiting for me.

Can I Take Your Order Please?

We live in a Burger King society. We want it our way, right away. Due to our lack of patience, we often miss out on God's best. Good things, God things, often take time. For some reason, we think time is something we don't have, and as a result, we end up forcing the wrong thing to happen. We force a marriage, only to get divorced. We take the wrong job, only to lose it. We buy a car we can't afford, only to overextend ourselves.

We do what we think is best, not what God said is best, and we suffer for it. Not only do we suffer but everyone around us suffers too.

Please let this sink in. There is a huge difference between what we think is best and what is best. Having a king was the worst thing for Israel but they thought it would be the best thing.

They settled for a cheap imitation of the real thing.

Saul Started It All

There was a wealthy, influential man named Kish from the tribe of Benjamin… His son Saul was the most handsome man in Israel—head and shoulders taller than anyone else in the land. (1 Samuel 9:1-2) NLT

At first glance, it looks promising. Saul is an impressive young man. He is tall and handsome. A man all the women want to be with and all the men want to be. The next two chapters tell us God's hand was upon Saul. So far, so good.

The story says Saul's dad lost some donkeys, so Saul and his men were sent to look for them. After a few days of no luck, Saul's servant spoke up, "There is a man of God who lives near here. Let's go talk to him. Maybe he knows where they are."

As they are on their way to meet Samuel, Samuel was on his way to meet them. He explains to them the donkeys had been found and then drops a bomb on Saul.

Samuel said, "I am here to tell you that you and your family are the focus of all Israel's hopes." (1 Samuel 9:20) NLT

What did you just say? It sounds like you just said something about me being someone's hope?

Preacher man, you've got the wrong man. The only hope I have is to find some donkeys.

Listen to Saul's reply, "But I'm only from the tribe of Benjamin, the smallest tribe in Israel, and my family is the least important of all the families of that tribe! Why are you talking like this to me?" (vs. 21)

Sound familiar? A little too similar to Gideon's reply.

But Samuel wasn't fazed and called for a banquet to be held in Saul's honor.

The next morning as Saul got up to leave, Samuel dropped another bomb.

"I have received a special message for you from God." Then he took a flask of olive oil and poured it over Saul's head. He kissed Saul and said, "I am doing this because the LORD has appointed you to be the ruler over Israel, his special possession."(1 Samuel 9:27-10:1) NLT

Can you imagine leaving to look for a bunch of donkeys and returning as an anointed king? Apparently, Saul couldn't either. Samuel reassures him these things are from the Lord. He even prophesies that several events will happen to confirm his word. Everything Samuel said would happen, happened.

As Saul turned and started to leave, God gave him a new heart, and all Samuel's signs were fulfilled that day. When Saul and his servant arrived at Gibeah, they saw a group of prophets coming toward them. Then the Spirit of God came powerfully upon Saul, and he, too, began to prophesy. (I Samuel 10:9-10) NLT

Wherefore Art Thou Saul?

After some time, Samuel calls the people together to officially anoint Saul as king. But there's a problem. They can't find Saul.

I'm not sure about you, but if there was one party I wasn't going to miss, it would be my coronation. I'm not gonna lie, I would have even helped plan the thing myself. First, get me downtown. Second, get me some old school Macy's Day floats. Third, I want banners hanging from the top to bottom floor on every building down Main Street. Fourth, get me the hottest DJ in town. I want him to collaborate with the band from University of Texas A&M and Grambling University. Fifth, get some candy falling from the sky. Sixth, get me some confetti, some balloons and some carnival people to sell my new merchandise. Seventh…I better stop here or you will get the wrong opinion of me.

Don't act like you wouldn't do the same. Don't believe me? Ladies, how involved were you in planning your wedding? How long did it take? How much did it cost? Would you have spent more if you could have? Would it have changed if you were royalty?

Men, you're not off the hook either. I've seen grown men act like kings when they beat a personal record at the gym or when they catch their biggest fish or when they shoot their biggest deer. Let's not pretend they don't celebrate when they finish a project they have been working on for years. I guarantee, if they could have an entourage, they would. Provide them a spot on the news, and they will gladly show up on time all cleaned up. I've even seen grown men cry like babies when their favorite player was voted into the Hall of Fame.

What I'm saying is, we are not going to miss our coronation.

But when they went looking for Saul he was gone. He must have been really gone, because the only person who could find him was God.

Want to know where they found him? Hiding with the baggage! Seriously, what is wrong with this guy?

Don't miss the importance of this moment. God had already spoken words of change over Saul's life and had already empowered him. But it didn't matter because Saul couldn't get past his insecurities. Even though he was given a new identity he still struggled with his old one.

When he should have been sitting on the throne, he was hiding under the baggage.

Meet You At the Baggage Claim

Paul wrote, "Therefore, if anyone is in Christ, the new creation has come: The old has gone, the new is here!" (2 Corinthians 5:17) NIV

If you have trusted in Jesus as your Savior, you have been changed. You have been given God's power and His Spirit lives within you. That is your new identity so please stop hiding under the old one. It is impossible to live under a new anointing if you are still living under old baggage.

Saul had been anointed king but was choosing to live as a slave.

This is important. Not everyone was anointed in the Old Testament as it was usually reserved for prophets, priests, or kings. But in the New Testament John writes, "You have been anointed by the Holy One." (1 John 2:20) ESV

Paul also tells the church at Corinth, "God…has anointed us." (2 Corinthians 1:21) ESV

This is exciting. In Christ we have been anointed. "Christ" comes from the Greek word Christos which means, "anointed one." Jesus Christ went up into heaven, sent down His Spirit to equip, indwell, empower and anoint you to accomplish your assignment.

The first person you have to convince this is true is you.

I challenge you to wake up every morning and say to yourself, "I am anointed to accomplish my assignment."

Say it out loud.

"I am anointed to accomplish my assignment."

Now say, "My assignment."

Not the one my mom has for me. Not the one my mother-in-law wants for me, but the one God has given to me.

If you don't know who you are, people will gladly tell you who you are not.

If you don't know your calling, other people will be glad to give you one.

Before you know it they will be the people you are trying to please.

Eventually Saul's insecurities became his death certificate.

The voice of the crowd began to drown out the voice of God.

When this happens, it never ends well.

First Day Jitters

After Saul is anointed king he goes back to work and everyone heads home, with the exception of a few men. Not long after, King Nahash, the Ammonite, rides into town and threatens to kill the Israelites. He even threw in a nice consolation price, "If you surrender, we won't kill, but we will gouge out your right eye."

How's that for a first day on the job?

Remember, Saul had already been anointed king and the Spirit of God had already come upon him. He sends a message to the people of Israel and they rally together. God gave them the strength to slaughter the enemy. The people were so excited they had won the battle, they anointed Saul as king a second time.

This time he showed up.

Now that Saul has everything under control, Samuel decides to retire. Just as he retires, Saul's son Jonathan picks a fight with the Philistines. What happens next defines his reign.

The Philistines loved to fight, but the Israelites didn't. They were so scared they hid in caves, rocks, tombs, and cisterns. Any place they could find a hole big enough to crawl in, they did. In his own words, Saul saw the men scattering and knew that if he didn't act soon, he would lose the troops.

In a moment of desperation, he seeks Samuel's help. After seven days of Samuel's absence, Saul took matters into his own hands and offered his own sacrifice to the Lord. He was willing to break the law in order to appease the people. Once again, he is driven by his insecurity that started a downward spiral of disobedience.

Samuel shows up just as the ceremony is coming to an end. He is furious. He prophesies the kingdom will be ripped from Saul. After several more blatant acts of rebellion, Saul admits to Samuel, "I have sinned. I have disobeyed your instructions and the LORD's command, for I was afraid of the people and did what they demanded." (1 Samuel 15:24) NLT

There it is. The fear of man is now sitting on the throne of Saul's heart.

It is impossible to please people and God at the same time.

The Apostle Paul wrote to the Church of Galatia, "If pleasing people were my goal, I would not be Christ's servant." (Galatians 1:10) NLT

This is where the tension lies. Most of us know we are different and that scares us. It certainly scares me.

No one wants to feel like they don't belong. It's just easier to blend in than stand out because standing out makes you a target.

If anyone knew this it was Saul. He had been standing out his entire life. The Bible says on multiple occasions that he was head and shoulders above the rest.

As soon as God calls you out, people start calling you out.

Who really wants to be called out?

That involves a separation and we have already established we are born with an innate desire to fit in. Therein lies the dilemma. We have a desire to stand out and be used by God, but fitting in feels so much better.

What if people don't like me? What if we are laughed at or made fun of for being different?

I don't want that for my kids and I doubt you do either.

Even though we post things like, "You laugh at me because I'm different. I laugh at you because you are all the same," the truth is, it's a lie. We would love for it to be true, but it's not.

I have rarely, if ever, had someone come into my office and say, "I'm so glad I am different. In fact, I don't need counseling, I just wanted to stop by and say, 'Praise the Lord, I have never found a place for me to fit in!'"

I hear the exact opposite almost on a weekly basis. "Pastor, what's wrong with me? I don't seem to fit in anywhere." No matter how many times I tell them to embrace their uniqueness because that's what makes them wonderful, they just want to fit in.

Everyone wants to belong. We even have it on the front doors of our church, "You belong here." However, the moment we feel we don't belong, we're out.

Me Too

I believe if you really want to help someone, start by saying, "Me too," not, "You should." It is better to be real than relevant. Plus, I have found if you speak to people's hurts, you will never lack an audience. Whether you are a saint, skeptic or sinner, everyone has common life events, experiences and emotions. My goal in the first five minutes of any sermon is to get you to shake your head in agreement. Regardless of who you are or where you have come from, if I can get you to shake your head in agreement with me, then we can go somewhere together.

I moved to Arizona to get away. I was tired of living in Tulsa. Don't get me wrong, it's a great place to raise a family, but not my family. Tulsa is where both my wife and I grew up and our families still live there. As I stated earlier, I pastored a church that took the best out of me. During that time my parents, who were members of my church, divorced after twenty-nine years of marriage. I was heartbroken. My wife's parents divorced when she was young so this now meant my children would never remember any of their grandparents being married.

I want to honor my family and don't feel it is necessary to speak negatively about them. However, after my parents' divorce things started unraveling and I just wanted to get away. I didn't really care where I went as long as people would have to call before they visit. The only place I didn't really care to move was Arizona. Who says God doesn't have a sense of humor?

One day I received a phone call from my former Youth Pastor. He had started a church in Arizona and was interested to know if I would be willing to come work for him. I said, "Nope. There is one place I would rather not live and that's Arizona." He promised that if I would come visit, I would change my mind. So I finally agreed to visit the second week of January. The worst that could happen was that I would get a free vacation out of it. The morning Amy and I flew out of Tulsa it was nineteen degrees with thirty mile an hour wind gusts and ice was on the way. When we landed in Arizona it was eighty degrees and without a cloud in the sky. Not a bad first impression.

Long story short, I fell in love with Arizona and moved there six months later. If anyone decided to come visit they would have to call at least two days in advance.

My original intention of moving to Arizona was to heal. I had been in ministry since I was eighteen and I was physically, emotionally, and spiritually tired.

The position I accepted in Arizona was Discipleship Pastor. For three years I had the time of my life! Every time something stressful came along I would give my opinion to the Lead Pastor if he asked and then go home to play with my wife and kids. I hadn't felt so joyful, so rested, and so at peace since high school.

February 4, 2012 everything changed. Our Lead Pastor, my former Youth Pastor, my closest friend in Arizona, was caught in an extramarital affair and forced to resign. I was heartbroken.

My first inclination was to pack up and move back home, but the Lord had other plans. The Executive Board asked if I would take the interim position until they could find someone and after a few months they asked if I would consider taking the job. At first I said, "Thanks, but no thanks."

When it came time to look for a Pastor, I went and hid under my baggage. I was scared and wasn't sure if I had what it took to be a Lead Pastor , a second time. I didn't want to go through the hurt and disappointment again because I wasn't so sure I would recover this time.

Do you want to know what my biggest insecurity was? I wasn't like the other pastors in town. I was different and I didn't feel like I belonged. I struggled trying to figure out how a country boy from Oklahoma could minister to people who were predominately from California. I know it sounds silly but it wasn't to me. My insecurity had me hiding under my baggage.

As you may know, I eventually accepted the position of Lead Pastor. I thought my insecurities would fade with time, but they didn't. In fact, they grew. The largest church I had ever been in was two hundred people and Mountain View was already at 500 when I became Pastor. In the first few months we grew to over 1,000. Within a few short years, we started averaging more people on a Sunday than I had in my entire home town growing up. Things were going great on the outside, but I was going crazy on the inside. Talk about conflict. I was grateful for God's goodness but terrified I was going to mess it up.

Two things happened that helped me tremendously.

One, I came across a little book I found in the bargain bin called *Purple Cow*, by Seth Godin. It was the best three dollars I ever spent. To save the details in hopes of you buying the book, let me just tell you the premise. Imagine taking your kids on a Sunday afternoon drive. Let's say your kids have lived their entire lives in the city. In fact, they have never been outside the city so everything is going to be a new learning experience. About twenty miles into the drive you come across a cow. Keep in mind, they have never seen a cow before. They scream, "Dad, dad, pull over. Let's take a picture of the cow." Because you are an awesome dad you agree, even though you know they might see up to a hundred cows that day.

Speaking of this. Could anyone please tell the tourists in Yellowstone National Park there are Buffalo inside the park too? In fact, they are around almost every corner so please stop blocking traffic and making the rest of us wait two hours just to get into the park. I promise, you will get your picture with a buffalo. There are plenty more to see!

Sorry, I had to get that off of my chest. I've been holding it in for five years.

Back to what I was saying. Chances are, after seeing close to a hundred cows, your kids are not going to keep asking you to pull over and take a picture. Trust me, once you have seen one cow, you have pretty much seen them all. They are not that interesting. They just stand there staring at you while chewing grass; it's what they do. Cows are possibly the most boring animal you could look at. Your kids will catch on fast so keep driving dad, keep driving.

However, if your kids ever saw a purple cow, well, that would certainly be something to talk about. That would be something even I would never forget.

The point of the book is, "What are you going to do to make your product, or even you, a purple cow?"

The second thing that helped me happened over a lunch meeting with a friend named Dave. I brought up that I was different. To be honest, I was actually just whining about my insecurities. He said, "Daniel, it sounds like you are trying to put a lid on what God can do through you. Have you ever thought that maybe God brought you here because you are different? Maybe He doesn't need you to be like everyone else because He already has them. Maybe He wants you to see your uniqueness as a strength, not as a weakness. Maybe Mountain View needs someone like you."

He was right, and at that moment I decided my uniqueness would be my strength. I wasn't weird, I was wonderful. I was going to come out from under my hiding and step into my calling. For the first time in fifteen years, I felt free to be the me God created me to be and nothing has ever been so liberating.

God has you right where He wants you.

Perhaps when you look in the mirror you see many excuses as to why you couldn't or shouldn't be the one who accomplishes something great. Perhaps you see all the reasons why somebody else is more qualified or more deserving. I get it because I felt the same way too. The problem is we have a tendency to hide behind these excuses. I am here to tell you, the days of allowing your excuses to hold you back are over. Our imperfections don't keep us from our destiny, they actually position us perfectly for it.

Don't center your life around self-preservation.

In order to experience life to its fullest, there will come a time when you have to stop worrying about what people think.

Do you want to know where people pleasing takes you?

Saul…was filled with depression and fear. (1 Samuel 16:14) NLT

Saul becomes obsessed with David and overcome with depression. Why? Because the people loved David more.

His story ends in the most tragic of ways. He takes his own life. A tragic end to such a promising beginning. People pleasing makes you do crazy things. Please don't let this be you.

Let me end with a few questions:

Who are you trying to please?

What baggage are you hiding under?

Do you have any baggage you need to get rid of?

Do you need to embrace your uniqueness as a strength, not a weakness?

Sermon in a sentence: What you think is best for you may not be God's best for you.

CHAPTER 8

THE STORY OF DAVID

Have you ever thought you were weird? Just a little bit? I have. Not about you, about me. I have never met anyone like me, so I used to think that was a bad thing, but not anymore. In the last chapter we talked about our desire to belong. We all have a longing for belonging. Did you know that you can belong and still be different? You see, unity is not the same as uniformity. Uniformity says you have to look like us, talk like us, and dress like us to be one of us. Unity says we may look different, we may talk different, and we may dress differently, but that doesn't keep us from being on the same team. This chapter is all about learning to leverage our uniqueness. Just because you are weird doesn't mean there is something wrong with you; it means there is something wonderful about you.

I don't think we were born to be "norm." Normal is boring. Normal isn't even working anymore. Normal is divorced, bankrupt and depressed. Who wants to be normal?

As I told you in the last chapter it took me a while to understand this.

God Loves Variety

It doesn't take a rocket scientist to know God loves variety. Go to the zoo or turn on the Discovery channel and you will see very quickly God loves diversity. Animals come in all shapes, sizes, colors, and kinds. There are over 300,000 species of beetles, 10,000 species of birds, 7,500 varieties of apples and 340 breeds of dogs. Isn't that creative overkill? Couldn't we have gotten along just fine with 50,000 species of beetles or 5,000 species of birds? I think so but as the master Creator and Artist, God loves variety.

He likes variety in people too. Go to the airport and people watch. If the airport is too far, go to the mall or Walmart or the county fair and you will see people come in all shapes and sizes, colors and kinds.

No matter how different these people are, one thing is for certain. God created them all.

God made trees and plants, bees and ants, fleas, seas, knees and peas, bumblebees and chimpanzees, and birds in the sky who have the power to fly. Some are wild and some are pets, but when He made you and I in His image, well, that's as good as it gets!

We are His crowning creation. We are not one in a million, we are one in seven billion. There never has been, and never will be, anyone else like you. Rick Warren says, "Uniqueness is not just a virtue, but a responsibility. You owe it to God and yourself, to be yourself. You were created to worship God in a way that no one else can. One of the ways you do that is by living your life in a way that no one else can. Fulfilling your destiny starts with discovering your identity."

Therein lies the challenge. Most of us live our entire lives as strangers to ourselves. We know more about others than we know about ourselves, and as a result our true identities get buried beneath the mistakes we've made, the insecurities we've acquired and the lies we've believed. We have become uncomfortable in our own skin. We spend far too much emotional, relational and spiritual energy trying to be someone we are not. Why? Because it's easier and somehow we think it's safer. It's not just that we are lying to ourselves, we are also losing ourselves.

The good news is, it's never too late to be who we were created to be!

If there was anyone who understood what it meant to embrace your uniqueness it was David.

Listen to how David is described.

"One of Jesse's sons…is a talented harp player and he is a brave warrior, a man of war." (1 Samuel 16:18) NLT

Read that line again.

Not Like the Other

When I was a child, my granny babysat me in the summer. Every morning she would allow me to watch cartoons and *Sesame Street.* I loved *Sesame Street*; in particular, I loved Bert and Ernie. Ernie used to play a game called, *One of These Things is Not Like the Other.*

Remember that game? For those of you who missed out on the fun, allow me to explain it. Viewers were shown a group of four items, one of which was different than the other three. It was our job as a viewer to identify the item that didn't belong.

For instance, there may be four bowls of cereal on the table. All four bowls have the same type of cereal, but one bowl is much larger than the others. Believe it or not, sometimes the most obvious thing is completely invisible.

Did you catch what was different about David?

David was described as a talented harpist and a brave warrior.

I understand I was raised differently than most people, but from where I come from, you don't normally put those two together.

"Hey man, you know David? Do you think you can take him?" "No way dude, I heard he plays a mean harp."

Make sense now?

David was different. He was mean on the strings and keen with a sling. He was also courageous and compassionate. He was kind and he could kill you. He worshiped and he worried. He was a man after God's own heart and took the desire of Uriah's heart. He was a man of extremes.

Have you ever read the book of Psalms? In one sentence he asks God to kill his enemies, the next he talks about the gracious hand of God. He was spiritually schizophrenic on the very same page. David was weird y'all!

However, it was his uniqueness that gained him favor. Being a harpist gave him the platform to stand before the king and being a warrior gave him the courage to stand before a giant. If he was just a warrior, he would never have had access to Saul. If he was just a harpist, he would have been destroyed by Goliath because we all know you can't sing a giant to sleep.

Maybe you wonder why you are the way you are. Have you ever thought God wants to work through your uniqueness? Maybe He allows insecurities so you can depend upon Him more. Maybe you have a tendency to worry so you will pray more. Maybe you have fears so you can take greater steps of faith. Maybe He made me bald so I wouldn't end up like Samson. Maybe I don't have a polished tongue so I would develop a passionate heart. Maybe God allowed my hurts so I could help heal others. Maybe He allowed conflicts so we could develop our character and strengthen our courage to carry out our future calling.

Maybe you think you are weird and maybe that's just what God wants to use to change the world.

Nothing is ever wasted in God's economy.

God needed a harpist and a warrior.

When you consider the circumstances of your life it is easy to assume you are nothing special. Just another person in a long line of sameness, but nothing could be further from the truth. The God of this universe personally wove you together and it is no accident you are the way you are.

God created mankind in his own image, in the image of God he created them; male and female he created them. (Genesis 1:27) NIV

For you created my inmost being; you knit me together in my mother's womb. I praise you because I am fearfully and wonderfully made; your works are wonderful, I know that full well. My frame was not hidden from you when I was made in the secret place, when I was woven together in the depths of the earth. (Psalm 139:13-15) NIV

Your hands shaped me and made me. (Job 10:8) NIV

From these verses we learn there is no one else like you. There never has been and there never will be. God doesn't create copies, He only creates originals. Why would He go to all that trouble? Because He knows how special you are. Did you know your body has about 37 trillion cells? If you stretched your DNA cells out, end to end, they'd stretch over 10 billion miles. The moon is 250,000 miles away, so your DNA would stretch to the moon and back almost 1,500 times. The sun is 93,000,000 miles away, so your DNA would reach the sun and back four times!

Your uniqueness is not weakness. Your uniqueness is what makes you wonderfully complex!

Rick Warren says, "The reason why we are so unique is because there is something God wants you to do that only you can do!"

The Hebrew word for create is bara. It literally means He lovingly shaped you together like a potter shapes clay.

Isn't that what Isaiah said about you?

We are the clay, and you are our potter; we are all the work of your hand. (Isaiah 64:8) ESV

God lovingly took the time to create you, and He did it for a reason and specific purpose. There is something you offer to the world that only you can offer to the world.

I don't want you to miss it.

Train Up a Child

I was brought up in a weird environment. My parents raised us boys in a very conservative Baptist church. It was a hell, fire, and brimstone type place. Suits, ties, dresses past knees, and King James Version of the Bible only. David said we should be glad when we go to the house of God, but I have to be honest, I was scared to death. As a little boy I would lie awake all night thinking about eternity. I wanted to be saved so I didn't go to hell, but I didn't want to go to heaven because I thought it would be like my church…forever. Talk about a conflict.

Our home was the opposite. My mom did her best to instill good Christian values in us, but my dad on the other hand, let's just say he did his best. I love my dad and he is one of my personal heroes, but he was an enigma. He would cuss one minute and pray the next. He would watch questionable shows at night, but his truck was always tuned to Jimmy Swaggart's radio program in the morning. I never could quite figure him out.

Truthfully, has anyone else heard of their dad getting into a fist fight at the gas station in a three piece suit after church, only to make it back in time for choir practice? Surely I am not the only one. Maybe by now you can see why I am so conflicted. I hate even writing this, but my dad's language wasn't the best either. He would often use racist terms, yet he was always the first to help those different than him. If he had a dollar he would give it. If he could meet their need he would meet it. If they needed a place to stay he would make sure it happened. He was hard to understand. He could be so mean one minute and so compassionate the next.

I get the idea that David's home wasn't perfect either.

New King in Town

After Saul's disobedience, Samuel is tasked with anointing a new king and was sent to a man named Jesse. Jesse was instructed to bring all of his boys in front of Samuel. At some point in the Mr. Israel pageant God would reveal which of the sons would be the next king of Israel. When they arrived, Samuel took one look at Eliab and thought, "Surely this is the LORD's anointed!"

He must have been a fine looking young man to have the old prophet saying, "You had me at hello!"

But God was doing something different.

What we see is not always what He is looking at.

But the LORD said to Samuel, "Don't judge by his appearance or height, for I have rejected him. The LORD doesn't see things the way you see them. People judge by outward appearance, but the LORD looks at the heart." (1 Samuel 16:7) NLT

I am so glad that God doesn't see things the way we see them. Looks can be deceiving. I've counseled too many couples who thought they were marrying an angel only to find out they were the devil in disguise.

Seven of Jesse's sons passed in front of Samuel and each time God said, "No." Finally Samuel asked, "Are these all the sons you have?" Jesse's reply is crazy, "Well, there is still the youngest, but he's out in the fields watching the sheep and goats." The word he chooses to describe David is least, runt. Samuel said, "Send for him at once. We will not sit down to eat until he arrives." (vs. 11)

Parents, what would it have hurt to have invited David? At least he could watch the pageant and see one of his older brothers crowned king. For goodness sake, can we at least put him in the family photo?

Whatever the reason, David was pretty much an afterthought. This is significant because the number seven in the Bible means perfect or complete. That's what Jesse thought so he assumed his first seven boys were all that he needed to bring before God. Again, God was doing something different. The number eight means new beginnings and David was the eighth son.

Jesse's afterthought was God's forethought.

David's brothers looked good outwardly, but God was looking for someone who looked good internally.

All Gear, No Game

For a few years my son played basketball. He has always been big for his age so he looked like a menacing force in the paint, but he was not. He's too much like his mother and his compassion is greater than his passion. Every year he wanted to get the new Kobe's, new MJ's, new KD's, or whatever else was in style at the time. There was no way I was going to spend that kind of money on a few months of YMCA basketball. My philosophy is that you don't get the gear until you get the game. We've all seen those kids who show up with the new shoes, new socks, new wristbands, new headband, new elbow sleeve and new man tights. They look like a baller, but they play like a prima donna, all gear and no game.

David's brothers looked the part, but apparently they didn't have the heart. God wanted someone who had both. Sadly, that's not what most people pay attention to. We look at what can be seen and as a result, many of us are often left on the outside looking in.

Let me remind you that just because you are an afterthought in your family's eyes, your coach's eyes, your spouse's eyes, or your boss's eyes, it does not mean you are an afterthought in God's.

The ones who are often cast out by men are often called out by God.

Someone needs to hear this today because you have been overlooked and underappreciated your entire life. No one notices all the hard work you put in and no one appreciates all you do.

It is easy to get a complex during this time. No one cares about me, no one likes me, everybody hates me, so I guess I'll go eat worms. God doesn't look at what we look at. He looks within.

You may not be visible but that doesn't mean you are not valuable.

If they held an election for the next king, David wouldn't have even made the ballot. Good thing God doesn't consult nominating committees or work through a democratic process.

God works through an anointing.

He tells Samuel, "Just because you don't see it, doesn't mean I don't see it. Just because he is on Jesse's bench doesn't mean he can't be in my starting lineup. He may be left out by men, but he's about to be called out by Me. Anoint David, the little scrawny runt, whose voice hasn't quite lowered yet, as the next king of Israel. I need someone who is a little weird. I need a warrior and a worshiper."

If you feel unloved by your parents, unnoticed by your kids, unseen by your boss, or ignored by your spouse, I need you to know invisibility is not an indication of unimportance. David was not forgotten, he was just hidden, because you hide stuff you really care about.

Hide the Oreos

I grew up in a house full of boys. One of us, or all three of us, always had a friend over. My mom did her best to keep the house stocked with food, but with this many boys in the house it was very hard to do. We rarely had sweets in the pantry because they never made it that far.

One thing you need to know about me is that I love candy. Love might be an understatement. I am addicted to candy. Candy is my Achilles heel.

I would say I am an angel most of the time, but if you touch my candy, I can turn into the devil real quick.

Anytime I was fortunate enough to score some candy I would hide it. Not only would I hide the candy, but I would hide the good snacks too. I may have been a sinner for hiding the good stuff, but I was also smart. I liked to go with my mother to the grocery store. She thought I liked the companionship, but I went because I liked knowing what snacks we were buying. It was all part of my evil scheme to trick my brothers into staying away from the good snacks and candy.

Here was the plan. For every good snack my mom would put in the cart, I would sneak in a not so good snack too. For instance, if she bought Oreos, I would throw in some Great Value Twist and Shouts. If she bought Cheetos, I would sneak in some Cheez Doodles. Along with every good treat I would sneak in a not so good treat. If I was feeling extra ornery, I would sneak in some fat free stuff too. When we got home I made sure I helped unload the groceries. I would stock the panty by putting the not so good stuff front and center. Why would I go to all this trouble? I was distracting my brothers and their friends from looking for the good stuff.

Just because something is visible does not mean it is valuable. Sometimes the more invisible it is, the more valuable it is.

I like to think God hides the good stuff until it's ready to be revealed. Moses was hidden, Gideon was hiding, and John the Baptist came out of nowhere.

In other words, stop wasting time trying to get people to notice you.

God sees you and will reveal you when He is ready.

Miser and Misery

I like to buy my wife nice things, but it wasn't always this way. The first few years of marriage I did not know how to properly treat my rib. I was a miser and I'm pretty sure she was in misery. One day she asked if we could budget in a new pair of jeans. We were young and broke so we couldn't afford anything too expensive. I told her the budget would have to be under twenty dollars. When she told me how much her jeans normally cost, I laughed. My mom bought our Big-n-Huskies at Walmart for ten dollars, and if my dad got a bonus we may have gotten some at Old Navy for fifteen.

Nothing will top our arguments over haircuts though. My grandmother had always cut my hair, and if we were in a hurry, or grandma couldn't do it, we would go to the local barber shop. My mom tried to avoid this option because the smoke was so thick and language was so bad she thought it would damage us forever. I guess she had forgotten what our family reunions were like!

Since my haircuts were either free or cheap, I almost died when Amy told me how much a typical women's haircut cost.

But everything changed after the birth of my daughter. The Lord revealed to me that my daughter would probably marry someone just like me. That was a scary thought and it made me realize that Amy was someone's daughter too. In fact, the Lord showed me she was His daughter and I needed to start treating her accordingly. So from that moment on, I began to budget in spoiling my wife. I didn't want my wife to become bitter and I didn't want my daughter to marry a bum. Amy has never expected it, nor asked for it, but she is absolutely worth it, and my daughter is too!

Honey, I Bought You a Dress

One day I was walking through the mall and saw a dress I thought Amy would like. I always keep her sizes and a list of her favorite things in my wallet. That way if I see a bargain, I get it. When I gave the dress to Amy she said she loved it and I believed her. The problem is, she never wore it. After a few months I started to get worried. Was it the wrong size? Does she not like it? Have I lost my taste?

Then one evening, as we were heading to an event, she walked out the door with the dress on. When I asked her why she had waited so long to wear it, she said she was saving it for something special. She liked it so much she was waiting for the right moment to show it off.

When you feel God has put you on a shelf or assumed He has forgotten about you, think again. It's not because you're not valuable or He doesn't love you, it's because He is saving you for something special. He is waiting for the right moment to show you off. He loves you so much He is hiding you. He is protecting and preserving you for something unique.

When that day comes I don't want you to miss it. I want you to be so secure of your identity in Christ that you are ready to step into your calling when called upon.

King Elvis

In 2002 RCA Records released an album called, *ELVIS: 30 #1 Hits*. It was a collection of the thirty number one hits sang by Elvis. It was an instant success and it went straight to the top of the charts in several countries. By 2003 the album had received certifications in more than fifteen regions and sold millions of copies worldwide. They even used old clips of Elvis performing to develop modern music videos. Amazingly, Elvis still had popularity worldwide nearly thirty years after his death.

Most people assume someone as popular as Elvis would have been satisfied with his life. But in spite of his enormous success, Elvis lived an unfulfilled, miserable life. Close friends say Elvis' fruitless search for significance led to his early death. His wife, Priscilla, is on record as saying, "He never came to terms with who he was meant to be or what his purpose in life was. He knew he was here for a reason, maybe to preach, maybe to serve, maybe to save, maybe to care for people. That agonizing desire was always with him because he knew he wasn't fulfilling it. So he'd go on stage, drink alcohol, and take drugs. He did whatever he could to keep his mind from thinking about it."

Elvis knew deep inside he had something unique to offer this world, but he never found what it was because he looked in all the wrong places. I don't want you to make the same mistake. I want you to discover who you are and embrace it.

There was a recent study of American college graduates who had to decide if they would take more money in a job they didn't like now, or do what they love now, and sacrifice the money in hopes of making it up later. The results were overwhelming. Those who chose to do what they loved first eventually made the money, while the ones who took the money first ended up quitting and bounced from job to job. They never could develop a passion for what they were doing no matter how much money they made, and over time they made considerably less money.

When you follow your heart's desire, you are much more likely to experience success.

Those who are often the most successful in their field are not always the smartest, most educated, or even the most gifted. They just found something they loved to do and went after it with all their heart. Charles Garfield wrote a bestselling book called *Peak Performance*. He studied everything from athletes to astronauts and found the biggest predictor of success was a strong passion for the work they were doing.

When you are doing what you love to do, you don't need anyone to motivate you. There's a natural enthusiasm so you won't need more rewards, more applause, or more supervision. Every day you will give your best because you love to do it whether you are paid or not.

Solomon, King David's son, said one of the greatest gifts in life is finding what we love to do and then doing it.

"My heart took delight in all my labor…" (Ecclesiastes 2:10) NIV

Do you delight in your work? If you don't, you are in the wrong job. God doesn't want life to be a drag, He wants life to be a delight. If your heart isn't in the work you're doing, it's likely dragging you down. Don't waste your life in a job that doesn't express who you were made to be. Sure, you may have to do it for a period of time, but don't let the season turn into a lifetime.

What are your passions? What would you do if they didn't pay you?

Preaching is not my profession, it's my passion. It's not what I do, it's who I am. I'll preach anywhere, anytime, about anything! I've been talking to people, leading people, and caring for people for as long as I can remember. Those who know me best and have known me the longest will tell you I'm the same Daniel I have always been. Why? Because this is not what I do, it's who I am.

I have found the more authentic I am, the more authority God gives me.

It's hard to be anything but you.

If you take the time to understand how you operate, it will reduce unwanted stress by allowing you to maximize what you're good at and not worry about the rest. If you don't have a heart for what you're doing, you're not going to be successful over the long haul because it will wear you down little by little each day.

What do you love to do and what are you good at?

I don't mean what your mama or your spouse tells you you're good at. What do multiple people tell you you're good at? What is something you do, and every time you do it, you experience positive results? Because in order to be successful over a long period of time you need both passion and productivity. This doesn't mean you won't have troubles or trials, but it does mean there should be development, progress, or advancement in whatever you are doing.

Keep in mind the issue isn't perfection, but progress. You don't have to be the best, just get better every day. It's the principle of passion and productivity.

Why am I bringing this up? David loved playing the harp, but David didn't get called to play the harp in front of the king because he was passionate about playing the harp. He got called to play the harp before the king because he was both passionate and productive.

Let us find a good musician to play the harp…"All right," Saul said. "Find me someone who plays well, and bring him here." One of the servants said to Saul, "One of Jesse's sons from Bethlehem is a talented harp player."…Whenever the spirit from God came on Saul, David would take up his lyre and play. Then relief would come to Saul; he would feel better. (1 Samuel 16:16-18, 23) NLT

It takes more than just passion to get the job done. David is described as a good musician who played well. In other words, his playing was productive. If it's for God, it ought to be good. When people come to church on Sundays they want me to be passionate, but they also want me to have studied. They want me to help them, educate them, challenge them, or stretch them. Why? Because they hope to be more productive.

How do you become more productive? Practice.

We Talking About Practice?

God deposited a gift within you, but that doesn't mean you will automatically get a return on that investment. You still have to develop the deposit and grow that gift. They didn't want just anyone who played music to stand before the king, they wanted the best. No one becomes the best by accident, it takes practice.

Experts say it takes about 10,000 hours of practice before you can be excellent at anything. How many hours do you think David practiced in order to be considered the best around? And let's not forget David was still a teenager. He could have been doing a million other things; he could have been watching the stars, talking on the rams horn, sheep tipping, and courting the ladies. Plus, he was a shepherd, which meant he had to lug his harp from pasture to pasture. It's not like he had his mom's minivan to help him carry it from field to field. He drug that old harp everywhere he went and practiced whenever he could find the time, so if he was ever called upon, he would be ready.

Not only did he practice his harp, but he apparently practiced his sling shot too. He was ready whether he was asked to play the king to sleep or called to kill a giant.

If you don't develop the deposit, create some disciplines, and be diligent, you may miss the destiny God has for you because you aren't ready when called upon.

God only works through what we are willing to work on.

If you work on your gifts, develop your deposit, and go through the daily grind, you will gain favor with God and man.

If you're saying, "I don't feel passionate about anything. There's nothing that gets me up in the morning saying, 'Woo-hoo, I get to do this today!,'" chances are you're not spending enough time with the Lord. The closer you get to the Lord, the more fully alive you become. If you want to become more passionate, spend more time in His Word, pray more, praise more and do a little self-discovery. If you want to find yourself, you've got to find God. Until you see yourself through His eyes, you'll never get a vision of who you can become. If you want to get to know yourself, you have to get to know God.

If you still don't have it figured out, go back and review your personal history. What were some of the things you used to enjoy doing? What gave you a sense of satisfaction? When did you feel most alive? When were you most productive?

Let me remind you that nothing is ever wasted in God's economy. Whether it be slaying the strings or slinging a stone, God needs a harpist and a warrior.

It's okay to be weird; that's what makes you so wonderful.

God made you a masterpiece, please don't let society make you insecure.

Sermon in a Sentence: My uniqueness isn't a weakness; it's what makes me wonderful.

CHAPTER 9

THE STORY OF SOLOMON

Have ever made a dumb decision? Dumb question, isn't it? We've all made dumb decisions. Like the time my wife asked me if she looked fat in those pants. I decided to tell her the truth when I should have lied. Honesty is not always the best policy, but sometimes acting like you didn't hear the question is. Or the time I decided to take a selfie while riding my minibike. Not smart! Almost tore my leg off on a park bench. Or the time I thought it would be good to shoot the windows out of my uncle's barn. Dumb. Lost a year's worth of sleep and lawn money. How about when I thought I could ski a double black diamond…on my first ever ski trip. Stupid. Lost my lunch, my pride and almost my life.

Decisions, Decisions, Decisions

Today we are faced with more decisions than ever before. A recent survey stated the average American adult makes about 35,000 decisions a day. With so many decisions each day how can we keep from making dumb ones? As you know, what may appear to be a small, insignificant decision, can have major life implications. Even the tiniest decision can completely change the direction of your life.

I did a quick Google search and found some of the worst decisions in United States history.

Sam Phillips sold his small recording company in 1955 to RCA records for $35,000, which included the contractual rights of a young man named Elvis Presley. He unknowingly forfeited royalties on more than one million records sold.

In 1936, Joe Schuster and Jerry Siegel sold the rights to Superman for $65 each.

In 1962, Dick Rowe, an executive at Decca Records, thought guitar groups were falling out of favor. So when the Beatles auditioned for Decca Records he refused to sign them.

In 1999, Excite was asked to purchase Google for $750,000. At the time, Excite was a highly trafficked search engine at the forefront of the dot-com boom. Excite CEO George Bell declined the offer. Today, Google is valued at $180 billion. Anyone remember Excite?

In 2000, Reed Hastings approached former Blockbuster CEO John Antioco and asked for $50 million to sell the company he founded, Netflix. He refused. Today, Netflix is worth over $32 billion dollars. Blockbuster only has one store left.

Bill Gates' high school girlfriend gave him an ultimatum, "It's me or the computer!" He chose the computer. What was her name again?

A thief in Boston attempted to steal two live Maine lobsters by sticking them down his pants.

Three prison guards went in together to purchase a trampoline for the inmates to use during recreational time. They were fired shortly thereafter when the inmates used the trampoline to jump over the fence.

I don't know about you, but I am tired of making dumb decisions and I am ready to start making wise ones. The problem is, I am often conflicted over which is which. Where can I go to find the wisdom to make the right decision?

Wisdom on the Go

A few years ago, the University of Tennessee football program was marred in controversy as many of their players had multiple off the field incidents. In an effort to help solve the problem, the university came up with an idea. Players were given an orange card small enough to fit in their wallets. The word THINK was printed in large letters across the top, followed by a series of questions designed to help the player make wise decisions in every circumstance. On the back of the card were the phone numbers of the coaching staff and team captains they could call at any time. They called it portable wisdom.

In the mid 1800's William Arnot published a commentary on the book of Proverbs. In his commentary he described the book of Proverbs as wisdom in portable form. I like that - wisdom in portable form.

The book of Proverbs is one my favorite books of the Bible. It is my "go to" book when I am looking for wisdom. There are thirty-one chapters, one for each day of the month. I read Billy Graham started each morning with a Psalm and Proverb. I figured if he thought it would be a wise thing to do, then it would be a very wise thing for me to do.

Proverbs is a collection of 915 sayings that provide food for thought and lessons for everyday living. It is one of the few books in the Bible that gives us its author, purpose, and theme in the first few verses. In fact, the first six verses contain the prologue for the entire book.

These are the proverbs of Solomon, David's son, King of Israel. Their purpose is to teach people wisdom and discipline, to help them understand the insights of the wise. Their purpose is to teach people to live disciplined and successful lives, to help them do what is right, just, and fair. These proverbs will give insight to the simple, knowledge and discernment to the young. Let the wise listen to these proverbs and become even wiser. Let those with understanding receive guidance by exploring the meaning in these proverbs and parables, the words of the wise and their riddles. (Proverbs 1:1-6) NIV

These verses explain that if you want to make good decisions, read God's Word. God's Word gives us wisdom for everyday living. God's Word prolongs our life by providing peace, protection, and prosperity. It keeps us away from the path of the wicked by providing discernment and discipline. It keeps us in right standing with others by teaching us how to walk in justice and fairness. It helps us hold our tongue so we win favor with God and our fellow man. It also gives intelligence to ordinary people while teaching the inexperienced the ropes.

Listen to how Proverbs 3:8 describes wisdom, "This will bring health to your body and nourishment to your bones." Forget Whole Foods and read the Bible. It's the best health plan there is!

All 915 verses of Proverbs are summed up in this one verse, "The fear of the LORD is the foundation of true knowledge, but fools despise wisdom and discipline." (Proverbs 1:7) NIV

The phrase, "fear of the Lord," is a common theme that runs throughout the book. The Hebrew word fear is yirah. It has a variety of applications, ranging from reverence and respect to panic and terror. In its most basic sense, fear is an emotion that warns us of danger and elicits a response that saves our lives. This is why the fear of the Lord is the beginning of wisdom. Without it, we have no reason for thinking eternal thoughts. As a result, we do what is right in the here and now. Without a fear of the Lord we have no foundation for morality and no framework for making sense of this world. Without a fear of the Lord there is no reference point for clear thinking and no power for clean living.

AW Tozer said, "A healthy fear of the Lord is the most satisfying emotion the human soul can know."

Without a healthy fear of the Lord we cannot understand the truths of God, the character of God, the graciousness of God, or even the glory of God. The fear of the Lord is the missing element in society. Proverbs hopes to restore that. So if you want wisdom to make the right decisions, learn to fear God and learn to think through issues in light of His Word.

Solomon, O Solomon, What Went Wrong with You, O Solomon?

Solomon is the predominant author of Proverbs and is David's second son from Bathsheba. Solomon was actually the seventeenth of David's nineteen sons. This hardly made him the most likely son to succeed his father as king. However, through the influence of his mother, and the support of Nathan the prophet, Solomon was named the third king of Israel in 961 BC. He was also known as Jedidiah, which meant beloved of the Lord. His forty year reign is regarded as Israel's golden age. It was an age of prosperity and national unity, though it did not end well. Truth is, it ended disastrously.

Solomon began to oppress the people, marry multiple wives, and introduced pagan worship. He also made some terrible political moves. He swiftly and ruthlessly established his power against his brother Adonijah, having him executed on a pretext. This act, along with the execution or banishment of Adonijah's supporters, created unnecessary military rivals on the northern edge of Israel. Adonijah's supporters became a major nuisance.

Despite it all, Solomon experienced a vision from God early in his reign. He was at the altar of Gibeon when an unprecedented event took place.

That night the LORD appeared to Solomon in a dream, and God said, "What do you want? Ask, and I will give it to you!" Solomon replied, "You showed faithful love to your servant my father, David, because he was honest and true and faithful to you. And you have continued your faithful love to him today by giving him a son to sit on his throne. Now, O LORD my God, you have made me king instead of my father, David, but I am like a little child who doesn't know his way around. And here I am in the midst of your own chosen people, a nation so great and numerous they cannot be counted! Give me an understanding heart so that I can govern your people well and know the difference between right and wrong. For who by himself is able to govern this great people of yours?" The Lord was pleased that Solomon had asked for wisdom. So God replied, "Because you have asked for wisdom in governing my people with justice and have not asked for a long life or wealth or the death of your enemies— I will give you what you asked for! I will give you a wise and understanding heart such as no one else has had or ever will have! And I will also give you what you did not ask for— riches and fame! No other king in all the world will be compared to you for the rest of your life!" (1 Kings 3:5-13) NLT

You Can Have Whatever You Like

We've all played the three wishes game. The game where a genie pops out of a bottle and says, "Ask for whatever you wish and your wishes will come true." There is always one smart mouth in the group who says, "My first wish is for three more wishes!" Use your imagination please, not your sarcasm. Thank you.

Seriously, if you could ask God for anything and it was a guarantee He would do it, what would you ask for?

Solomon actually had that opportunity. Instead of asking for fame or fortune, Solomon asks for wisdom. The Lord was so pleased with his request He decided to give Solomon wisdom and wealth, and not just everyday wisdom. The Bible says his wisdom surpassed all the people on the earth; not in one area, but in every area of life. In fact, foreign leaders traveled from all over the world to learn from him. Make no mistake, Solomon had wisdom. However, what he did not have was discernment. Discernment acts as a means of protection that guards us from being deceived spiritually.

Just Say No

The Book of Deuteronomy warned the kings of Israel not to do three things:

1. Acquire a great number of horses for himself.

2. Acquire multiple wives.

3. Acquire large amounts of silver and gold.

Solomon broke all three of these commands.

He married multiple women, 700 wives and 300 concubines to be exact.

He multiplied gold and silver. His worth has been estimated at $2.1 trillion. The Bible states King Solomon held a fortune that dwarfed any and every person who lived before him. His reign lasted forty years, and each year he received twenty-five tons of gold. One ton of gold can be worth as much as $60 million dollars. Twenty-five tons times forty years amounts to $60,000,000,000, not to mention his additional income derived from business, trade, and the annual tribute paid to him by the kings and governors of Arabia. King Solomon was reportedly so rich that his immense wealth caused silver to be considered of little value and as common as rocks.

He also acquired multiple horses. Solomon amassed a huge army, including 12,000 horsemen and 1,400 charioteers, even though they never went to war during his reign.

How could a man so wise be so dumb? Was it greed? Yes. Was it the desire for power? Yes. Was it lust? Clearly. Did greed, power and lust cause him to make compromises with the world? Without a doubt. And as a result, he ever so slowly began to turn from God.

The great and wise Solomon died smothered in wealth, sex and power. Talk about a conflicted soul!

Where Did It Go Wrong?

A recent survey asked 8,000 students at forty-eight colleges what they considered to be "very important" to them. The study conducted by John Hopkins University reported that sixteen percent of the students answered, "making a lot of money." Not surprising, but more than seventy-five percent said their first goal was, "finding purpose and meaning in life."

Psychologist Carl Jung said a third of all psychiatric cases are not suffering from a clinically definable neurosis, but from the senselessness and emptiness of their lives.

Hugh Moorhead, philosophy professor at Northeastern University, wrote to 250 philosophers, scientists, writers and intellectuals asking a simple question, "What is the meaning of life?" Some offered their best guess, others admitted they made up an answer, and most admitted they had no idea. Several even responded back asking Moorhead if he had discovered the purpose of life.

Toward the end of his life Solomon asked the same question, "What is the purpose of life? Is happiness even a possibility? Is joy a myth? Have I been looking in the wrong places?"

Solomon should have known the answer to these questions. He should have been the, "happily ever after," story, but he wasn't. He continually compromised his integrity, therefore drifting him farther and farther away from his destiny. The farther he drifted from his destiny, the greater the emptiness he felt.

In the twilight of his life he wrote two books, Proverbs and Ecclesiastes. As he looks back upon his youth he revisits the wreckage of a wasted life.

Someone once said, "It's what we learn after we know it all that really counts."

Solomon became wise after he realized how dumb he really was.

In Ecclesiastes he uses the phrase, "under the sun," twenty-five times. This phrase is the key to his folly. He never could grasp what it meant to look at life in the eternal sense. He was always looking at what was happening in the here and now, what was going on under the sun.

It is easy to lose sight of eternity when we are constantly distracted by the temporary.

Exercise Bikes

When you only look at the world in its here and now, it is easy to become discouraged and develop the philosophy of living in the moment. However, when you live in the moment, it is easy to lose sight of life's meaning. If you are trying to find happiness apart from God, you will end up feeling that everything in life is meaningless. The course of this life is the same, the circle of the sun is the same, the circuits of the winds are the same, and the cycle of water is the same. It's like life is one giant exercise bike. We get up, go to work, come home, eat dinner, watch TV, and go to bed. We do this day after day until retirement. We spend a lot of energy, but never really accomplish much. It's frustrating. Nothing changes and nothing is gained. We come and go and the world keeps spinning.

Bed Pillows

I hate making the bed. I just can't see the point to it. Even if I have guests, they have no business in my room. They are welcome in my house, but stay out of my room. Making the bed is as useless as any activity under the sun. But for some reason, my mother made me do it every day and my wife prefers I do it every day.

I don't mind doing housework. I'll get on my knees and mop the floor by hand. Laundry, no problem. Dishes, easy. Vacuuming, relaxing. Dusting, refreshing. Making the bed, annoying.

To top it off, my wife has ten pillows on our bed. How do I know? I counted them.

The reason I don't like to make the bed and put the hundred million bed pillows back on is because I am going to be getting back in it later that night. You make the bed and then you unmake it. You take the pillows off and then you put them back on. You do this day after day until you die. It's annoying.

Solomon thought life was a lot like bed pillows and exercise bikes. I know what he's talking about.

Test Time

Solomon decides to conduct a test. He has the means, so why not experience everything the world has to offer and see if anything is really meaningful? The report of his findings are found in Ecclesiastes.

Test 1: The Quest for Wisdom

I, the Teacher, was king of Israel, and I lived in Jerusalem. I devoted myself to search for understanding and to explore by wisdom everything being done under heaven. I soon discovered that God has dealt a tragic existence to the human race. I observed everything going on under the sun, and really, it is all meaningless—like chasing the wind. What is wrong cannot be made right. What is missing cannot be recovered. I said to myself, "Look, I am wiser than any of the kings who ruled in Jerusalem before me. I have greater wisdom and knowledge than any of them." So I set out to learn everything from wisdom to madness and folly. But I learned firsthand that pursuing all this is like chasing the wind. The greater my wisdom, the greater my grief. To increase knowledge only increases sorrow. (Ecclesiastes 1:12-18) NLT

Solomon was confused. He pursued education, exploration and experimentation like no man before him, but the more he mastered these fields, the emptier it seemed, and the less he seemed to know.

TS Eliot said, "All knowledge brings us nearer to our ignorance." In other words, the more we learn, the more we realize the less we actually know.

Karen Cheng was called a wonder woman, for she achieved a perfect score on both sections of her SAT test and the rigorous Berkeley acceptance exam. This is a staggering intellectual feat as no one had done this before. Karen had an unquenchable thirst for knowledge and an uncanny ability to retain whatever she read. She could answer any question thrown her way…well, almost any question. One day a reporter stumped her with a question she could not answer, "What is the meaning of life?" Karen was stunned, so she replied, "I have no idea. I would love to know myself."

Solomon discovered that apart from God nothing is gained under the sun. It is like chasing the wind. It may fill your sails for a while, but the moment you try to bottle it up, it's gone.

Test 2: The Quest for Pleasure

Solomon goes from being an eager college student who wants to learn all he can, to an eager college frat boy who wants to party all he can.

I said to myself, "Come on, let's try pleasure. Let's look for the 'good things' in life." But I found that this, too, was meaningless. So I said, "Laughter is silly. What good does it do to seek pleasure?" (Ecclesiastes 2:1-2) NLT

You can almost visualize the scene. His palace resembled a tenth century version of Las Vegas' Caesars Palace; big city, bright lights, bands, Benjamin's, bubbly and babes. The possibilities for pleasure were endless. The problem is, the mornings after all looked the same.

He came to the realization that you can only laugh and party so much before it all seems foolish. Pleasure is only a temporary intermission from the true pain you are hiding.

Many of you can empathize with Solomon. You've been down the road of pleasure only to find it leads nowhere. So Solomon did what many people do to numb the pain; he turned to substance abuse.

After much thought, I decided to cheer myself with wine. And while still seeking wisdom, I clutched at foolishness. In this way, I tried to experience the only happiness most people find during their brief life in this world. (vs. 3)

The problem with substance abuse is that it is fleeting and artificial, and the more you consume the more you need to feel its effects. What starts out as fun becomes an addiction, what becomes an addiction becomes a sickness, and what becomes a sickness eventually leads to death. Whether it's your health, your wealth, your relationships, or your job, something always dies when we try to numb the pain with a substance.

Test 3: The Quest for Wealth

Hippiness of the 60's led to hedonism of the 70's; hedonism of the 70's led to yuppieism of the 80's; yuppieism of the 80's led to materialism of the 90's.

I also tried to find meaning by building huge homes for myself and by planting beautiful vineyards. I made gardens and parks, filling them with all kinds of fruit trees. I built reservoirs to collect the water to irrigate my many flourishing groves. I bought slaves, both men and women, and others were born into my household. I also owned large herds and flocks, more than any of the kings who had lived in Jerusalem before me. I collected great sums of silver and gold, the treasure of many kings and provinces. I hired wonderful singers, both men and women, and had many beautiful concubines. I had everything a man could desire! So I became greater than all who had lived in Jerusalem before me, and my wisdom never failed me. (vs. 4-9)

He drops out of school, parties hard, and now realizes it's time to get a job. He thinks, "If wisdom and wild living let me down, maybe I can go to work and build a legacy." The problem is, he is doing all of this for himself. Notice how he refers to himself fourteen times in just a few verses.

Is work a valid place to find meaning? It can be, but not if it's done for the wrong reason. Is marriage a place to find purpose? It can be, but not if you are in it for yourself.

If you look to find meaning in work but are only in it for the money, you will end up empty. If you get married for pleasure, you can marry 700 wives and have 300 concubines and still not be happy.

Ernest Hemingway was a twentieth century Renaissance man. He lived life to its fullest. He sipped champagne in Paris, hunted grizzly bears in Alaska, watched bull fights in Spain and harpooned fish in the Florida keys. He pursued everything under the sun yet he still stuck a shotgun in his mouth and pulled the trigger.

We want so badly to believe we can earn our ticket to happiness and that our proud accomplishments will lead us to distinction and significance. As Hemingway said, "We are after all, the captain of our souls."

Contrast that with what Jesus asked, "What shall it profit a man if he gains the whole world yet loses his soul?"

A life apart from God is no life at all. The saddest truth of Ecclesiastes is that Solomon addresses God, but never in a personal way. He never uses His name or calls Him Father. He is stuck under the sun.

He viewed God as a distant Creator who is out there somewhere but not involved in our life as a personal Savior.

If you don't know Jesus as your Savior, it is impossible to live a meaningful life. Look at those who acquired everything life has to offer - people like Michael Jackson, Prince, Chris Farley, Junior Seau, Elvis, Jimmy Hendrix, Marilyn Monroe, Kurt Cobain, and Robin Williams. They all achieved fame and acquired wealth but their lives ended in a pit of despair.

You need more than women, wisdom, and wealth. Maybe that's the answer. I need more.

Test 4: The Quest for More

John D. Rockefeller was once asked, "How much money is enough?" His reply, "Just a little bit more. I don't want to own all the land in the world, just the land that touches mine."

Survey after survey has shown the desire for financial gain is actually a happiness suppressant. Too many people climb the ladder of success only to find that when they get to the top there is nothing there.

Scholars who research happiness found the magical number for families to be happiest is around $75,000 a year. Below this number they feel they don't have enough to help their kids. Over it, they feel they have too much and that it's hurting their kids. Having the money and saying we won't is harder than not having the money and saying we can't.

"Anything I wanted, I would take. I denied myself no pleasure." (vs. 10)

Isn't this the American dream? Deny yourself nothing, follow your heart, and do whatever makes you happy.

Solomon denied himself nothing and gained nothing.

"As I looked at everything I had worked so hard to accomplish, it was all so meaningless—like chasing the wind. There was nothing really worthwhile anywhere." (vs. 11)

Success is a lot like cotton candy; it tastes good, but is a whole lot of empty calories.

What's the Point?

So I decided there is nothing better than to enjoy food and drink and to find satisfaction in work. Then I realized that these pleasures are from the hand of God. For who can eat or enjoy anything apart from him? (vs. 24-25)

Did you catch the key phrase in the tragedy of Solomon's life?

It's the phrase, "Apart from Him."

Apart from Him everything is meaningless, but in Him there is meaning. In Him there is joy. In Him there is gladness. In Him there is contentment. In Him there is purpose. In Him there is peace. In Him there is satisfaction. Apart from Him there is nothing, but in Him is everything you are looking for.

Eight times in this book we hear the same sentiment that we can find purpose under the sun, but it can only be found, "in Him."

We can enjoy our homes and families. We can enjoy the pleasure of recreation. We can enjoy a nice vacation. We can enjoy a nice meal with friends. We can enjoy our work and wealth, if these things are pursued in Him. It is only when we put these things in their proper place that we can enjoy them as they were meant to be enjoyed. They are an appetizer, and a good appetizer at that, but they are only preparing us for the main meal: a relationship with Him.

Those who know God can attest to the fact that apart from Him life is nothing, but in Him, life is everything we hoped it would be!

Grandpa Sol

Solomon packed a suitcase full of memories and the world's greatest treasures, but as he opens his suitcase he realizes he had forgotten the only thing that mattered.

It is possible to have a full suitcase, but when you reach your final destination you will realize the whole trip was meaningless if you don't have God.

In the next to last verse of Ecclesiastes Solomon wrote, "Here now is my final conclusion: Fear God and obey his commands, for this is everyone's duty." (Ecclesiastes 12:13) NLT

Two of Solomon's most prominent books say the most practical thing, "The fear of the LORD is the beginning of wisdom." (Proverbs 9:10) NIV

Wisdom is what he asked for and wisdom is what he finally received. But it didn't come through the things of man; it came through the fear of God.

Got Questions?

I would like to end this chapter by giving you a few questions to ask when trying to make a wise decision. I learned these questions many years ago from Pastor Rick Warren.

1. Is this in harmony with God's Word?

God's will is found in God's Word, so stop looking for a sign and start looking for a verse. God's will never contradicts God's Word. Situations may change but the principles of God's Word remain the same.

At the end of the day, you have to decide who is going to be the ultimate authority in your life. You really only have two choices – God's Word or man's word, scripture or society.

If you base your life on society, you're always going to be anxious because it changes every day. You will be conflicted about the decisions you make because you won't have a strong foundation, you'll have a shifting one.

Society wants you to believe there is no such thing as absolute truth, only circumstantial truth.

Let's play a game. Close your eyes and point north.

I am going to assume some of you think north is one way and others of you think it is another way? Who's right? Both of you are sincere in your belief, but only one can be right. If we think truth is based upon the conditions of our environment or feelings, we are going to end up lost half the time.

What allows us to find our way is knowing north is always north and south is always south. The earth is in constant motion, but this earth operates without chaos because there are certain absolutes. We can always count on certain things to be true. What if gravity changed every year or the laws of mathematics changed depending upon your professor? This world would be in chaos.

God set up the universe with certain laws for our benefit. When we cooperate with the principles of this universe life is easier, but if you reject, rebel, disobey, or ignore these principles, you're the one who gets hurt. The same is true with moral and spiritual laws.

Wisdom comes when we build our life on what God says, which never changes; not on what society says, which always changes.

2. Do I want other people to know?

If you're making a decision and worried other people may find out, then it is probably a bad decision. Bad decisions lead to secrets and you're only as healthy as your secrets allow you to be. Integrity says your public and private life match. Even if you fool everyone else, you can't fool yourself. A great question to ask is, "Can I do this with a clear conscience?" If you violate your conscious you will have to pay. My Great-grandmother Leola always said, "If you do what is right you can sleep at night, but if you do what is wrong you will toss and turn all night long."

What about the gray areas?

Paul wrote, "If you do anything you believe is not right, you are sinning." (Romans 14:23) NLT

This verse says when in doubt cut it out, or at least when in doubt work it out. There may be some things you can't do today, but through studying God's Word those things could change. I'm not talking about truths, I'm talking about gray areas. As you grow and mature in Christ so will your convictions.

3. Will this make me a better person?

As Christians we have an incredible amount of freedom, but just because you can do something doesn't mean you should.

Paul says, "Everything is permissible, but not everything is beneficial." (1 Corinthians 10:23) CSB

Most of the choices we make in life are not really between good and evil. I doubt you get up in the morning and ask, "Shall I read my Bible or become a thief? Should I pray or become a drug addict?" Those kinds of things don't cross your mind, or at least I hope not.

The issue is usually between what's good for you and what's best for you. Some things are not necessarily wrong, they're just not necessary. Most activities in life are morally neutral. There's nothing wrong with TV, movies, or the Internet, but you don't want your kids sitting in front of them all day. There's nothing wrong with sleeping in but you shouldn't do it every day.

I think we ask the wrong question. Instead of asking, "Is there anything wrong with this?" A better question to ask is, "Is this making me a better person?"

I'm on a lifelong pursuit of becoming better every day, so there are some things that aren't bad for me, they're just not best for me. In every situation I try to ask myself this question, "Is this making me better?"

4. Could this control my life?

No matter how fun something is, if it begins to dominate or control your life, your thoughts, your behavior, or your time, it is probably best to stay away from it. I have chosen not to drink alcohol. In fact, I have never had a drink of alcohol. Well, there was that one time my mom made me some whiskey, tea, and honey when I was only twelve. It was medicinal. At least that's what she told me.

Alcoholism runs in my family, so I have seen the negative effects of alcohol my entire life. This may surprise you, but I have never had a couple come in for marriage counseling and say, "Pastor, our marriage stunk, but the moment we started drinking together everything changed." I have never had that happen, nor heard of it happening. However, I do hear the exact opposite, "Alcohol destroyed our marriage and family."

I choose to stay away from alcohol because I can't become an alcoholic if I never have a drink.

Paul also said, "All things are lawful for me but I will not be controlled by anything." (1 Corinthians 6:12) NET

Why? Because whatever controls your life eventually becomes god of your life. The first commandment is, "You shall have no other gods before Me." God knew how easy it would be for us to do this.

Today there are over 2,000 classified addictions. How do you know if something's starting to control you? You think about it when you are alone. You worry about it. You talk about it. You have to do it.

If you're thinking, "That's not what I'm addicted to," it probably is.

Jesus is the only one that's worthy of control. Anything else we put in His place will eventually control our lives. That's why asking, "Could this become addicting or controlling?" is such an important question to consider when making difficult decisions.

5. Will this harm other people?

One of the biggest mistakes we make is assuming our actions don't impact others. Culture teaches us to think only of ourselves, but God expects us to think of the people around us. Everything we do affects other people. There is no such thing as, "I'm only hurting myself." Every parent knows little eyes are always watching and little ears are always listening. Because of this, you want to be careful. You are always influencing other people. Live a life that not only betters yourself, but those around you too.

6. Is this the best use of my time?

If you want to make the best of your life, you have to get control of your time. Your time is your life. You can always make more money, but you can't make more time. In essence, if you waste time, you're wasting your life. Always ask, "Is this the best use of my time?"

There are many things I choose not to do. Not because they're bad or I don't enjoy them. I've chosen not to do them because I want to maximize my time. I don't make time for everything or everyone and I don't think God expects me to.

A focused life is a powerful life. Successful people focus on what's important. Jesus did not get involved in trivial things. He stayed away from politics, He didn't heal everyone and He didn't preach to everyone. He knew what He came to do and didn't allow Himself to become distracted.

I understand you can't eliminate all the trivial things in life, but you can reduce them. That's the hard part, especially when you're tired. When you're tired, you don't do the best thing, you do the easy thing. If you want to make good decisions, get some rest!

I have learned the hard way that I will never know what God wants me to do until I stop doing what I shouldn't do. Then I can hear God tell me what I should do.

Stay Focused

Solomon never could stay focused. His endless pursuit of wealth, wisdom, wine and women robbed him of wisdom. What a dumb decision. Don't let that be you. Stay focused.

Let's end with some self-evaluation:

Are you being tempted to do something that is contrary to God's Word?

Are you exactly who you appear to be or are you living a double life?

Are you making decisions that are making you better?

Is anything out of control in your life? Your schedule? Your temper? Your habits? Your spending?

Are your actions hurting other people?

Are you investing your time on things that matter or on things that won't matter in five years, ten years or fifty years?

Sermon in a Sentence: God's will is found in God's Word, so stop looking for a sign and start looking for a verse.

SOLID ROCK BUT A STUMBLING BLOCK

CHAPTER 10
THE STORY OF PETER

For any child growing up in Oklahoma it is a rite of passage to learn the song, *Oh, What a Beautiful Mornin'* by Oscar Hammerstein II. It was, after all, the opening song in Rodgers and Hammerstein's classic, *Oklahoma!* When I hear Gordon MacRae sing these words it still gives me goosebumps…

Oh what a beautiful mornin'

Oh what a beautiful day

I've got a beautiful feelin'

Everything's going my way

Have you ever had one of those days? A day where you have a "beautiful feeling everything's going your way?" Sure you have. Your hair is on point, your eyebrows are on fleek and your clothes fit just right! They might be few and far between, but I know you have had at least a handful. Probably before you had kids, but that's for another book.

Believe it or not. I have even had a few days where I started out feeling incredible. I was ready to conquer the world, take on my fears, defeat my enemies and achieve my dreams. But by midmorning, my blue sky turned gray, my faith turned into fear, my joy turned into despair and my perfect hair got caught in a perfect storm. I started the day feeling like I could conquer the world only to have it end by wanting to crawl under a rock.

Nightmare After Christmas

I love Christmas. It has always been my favorite holiday and I love it even more now that I have kids. I have to be honest with you though, sometimes it's hard to get in the Christmas mood in Arizona. Arizona has two seasons, paradise and purgatory. Before I sound too whiney, I have to admit December in Arizona is absolutely perfect. However, every once in a while I would like to be forced to wear a jacket. I'm not down with wearing shorts and flip-flops on Christmas. A hoodie would be nice.

We have made a commitment at Mountain View to do everything we can to help people get into the Christmas spirit. We bring in snow, we build Santa's village, we transform our entire campus into a winter wonderland. It is incredible!

Because we have a K-8th grade and a preschool on campus, the entire month of December is filled with programs, plays and parties. Mountain View is the place to be at Christmas time and I love it.

I believe our Christmas Celebrations are some of the best in the valley and every year is better than the one before. We've had snow in the Auditorium, confetti cannons, ballet dancers, a gospel choir, a violinist, and just about everything else you can think of; even Santa and his elves make an appearance.

Due to the popularity, we host anywhere from six to eight Celebrations on Christmas Eve, in addition to our normal weekend Celebrations. One year I spoke ten times in three days. As a result, the Christmas season is not one of rest for our staff. We wrestle with the tension of loving Christmas but hating the stress it brings.

When my kids were younger, Amy and I felt the responsibility to have them around family on Christmas. That meant we got up early on Christmas morning to see what Santa brought before hitting the road to see what grandpa and grandma bought. When I say early I mean before Jesus was up, like 3 a.m.

Nothing is worth getting up that early for. I promise.

Sleep is already at a premium this time of year, at least for me. (Amy has a clear conscience and can sleep anywhere, anytime. My mind accelerates at bedtime.) I don't do well when I don't get sleep. I am the most like the devil when I am sleep deprived, impatient and irritable. For the next sixteen hours I get the privilege of listening to my kids fuss, fight and feud. Noah pesters Eva. Eva frustrates me. Amy sleeps through it all. It has become known as our annual holiday trip to hell.

Not only have I not slept much, I usually haven't eaten much either. The stress of the season causes my stomach to be in knots.

To top it off, I am also on edge because the weather is unpredictable. I am one situation away from losing it.

I love my family, but if there is one word to describe them, it would be Griswold-esque. Clark, Eddie and Edna have nothing on us.

The first time Amy met my extended family was Christmas. As we pulled into the drive way of my grandfather's house, my cousin's daughters were outside in their pretty dresses. Amy said, "Look how cute they are." As soon as she said it, one of them tackled the other one and a full on WWE wrestling match broke out in the front yard. Before we knew it there were at least fifteen to twenty cousins brawling it out in the front yard. Sadly, this was not a rare occurrence.

I'm not positive, but I'm pretty sure they wait an entire year to bring the craziness out. The holidays bring out the best in everyone, right?

As soon as I pull into the driveway and start unloading the car, the drama starts being unloaded on me. So and so blocked so and so on Facebook. She lost her job. He is back on the bottle. She left him. He cursed at her. They haven't talked to them in months. We are one big happy family.

One year it got so bad I had to drive to the other side of town to see my mother so no one else would know. Why? My father was mad at my mother. My mother was mad at my granny. My younger brother was mad at my older brother. My granny was mad at her sister. No one could be in the same room without WWIII breaking out. As a result, we are never able to stay in one place very long, so we spend half of our time driving from here to there.

I don't know what to say except, "It's Christmas, and we are all in misery!"

Here is the thing. It's not like this is a surprise. I know it is going to happen because it has happened my entire life. I try to prepare myself mentally, emotionally and spiritually. Amy and I even come up with code words to say when it's time to leave. "Mistletoe!"

But it never fails. No matter how much I pray, no matter how hard I try, every year I have a Clark Griswold meltdown moment.

The moment it happens, my mind is flooded with a million negative, self-defeating, shameful, condemning thoughts: "You are yelling at your wife just like your dad did. You are going to make Christmas miserable for your kids just like yours was. You call yourself a man of God? You can't even control your temper. You are a phony. You're a hypocrite. Things will never change. You're just like your dad and you always will be. Your wife is going to leave you and your kids are going to hate you."

It doesn't take much for me to be overcome with guilt, embarrassment and discouragement. I go from telling others how much God loves them by giving the gift of Jesus, to believing I am not even worthy to receive this gift myself.

I don't want it to happen. I don't plan on it happening. I pray, I fast and I think positive thoughts, but it happens anyway.

I am conflicted.

I love celebrating the birth of Jesus, but it sure is stressful. I go from the highest of highs to the lowest of lows and it all plays out in front of the ones I love the most.

It hurts deeply.

I'm sure you have felt this way too. Thank the Lord we are not the only ones.

A Conflicted Soul

The Apostle Peter is one of the most famous men in the Bible. At times he showed exceptional faith. Other times he showed almost no faith.

He was a man of both great triumphs and colossal failures.

A man whom Jesus called the Stone and Satan.

A man who declared Jesus to be the Son of God and then denied he knew the Son of God.

He was incredible one moment and despicable the next.

His life seems to be a paradox. He speaks before he thinks. He acts before he thinks. Sometimes he doesn't think at all. He was by nature brash, arrogant and undependable. He was carnal and spiritual; the original, "shock and awe," personality.

Despite all of this, God still called him, loved him, forgave him and used him to change the world.

Thank God for Peter, because Peter, more than any other person in the Bible, is someone we can relate to. At least, I can.

In fact, I believe there is a little bit of Peter in all of us.

The Gospel of John describes his first interaction with Jesus this way: Jesus looked at him and said, "You are Simon son of John. You will be called Cephas," (which, when translated, is Peter). (John 1:42) NIV

Jesus' first recorded words to Peter were, "I'm changing your name from Simon to Cephas, which means the 'Rock!'" Sorry Dwayne Johnson, there was another Rock before you.

From this point on, "Rock" was his name. The only time Jesus refers to him as Simon is when he's getting into trouble. This must be where our parents get it. Apparently, it's in their divine DNA to call us by our full name when we are in trouble.

Did you know Peter's name is mentioned in the New Testament more than any other name except Jesus? How cool is that?

Jesus also speaks directly to Peter more than any other person.

Peter is recorded as asking more questions than all the other disciples combined, and he answers more questions than all the other disciples combined. He was also the only one who had the guts to openly rebuke Jesus, therefore making him the one Jesus openly rebuked.

Most scholars believe the Gospel of Mark is actually based upon Peter's memoirs. It should be called the Gospel of Mark according to Peter.

According to history, Peter labored in Rome during the last portion of his life. Tradition says he was crucified upside down because he did not consider himself worthy enough to die in the same manner his Savior did. Saint Peter's Basilica in Rome is believed to be his burial site.

Matthew 16 reveals his conflicted soul best.

One moment he confesses Jesus as the Son of God and the next moment he is called Satan by the Son of God.

Peter, more than anyone else, teaches us that becoming the person God created us to be takes time.

His life is best summed up in a verse he penned toward the end of his life:

"Grow in the grace and knowledge of our Lord and Savior Jesus Christ." (2 Peter 3:18) NIV

That is exactly what he did. He grew.

Chicken Or the Egg

Life is full of questions. There are philosophical questions. What came first, the chicken or the egg? Did Adam have a navel? Where do forest rangers go to get away from it all? What do I do if I see an endangered animal eating an endangered plant? Can vegetarians eat animal crackers? Can an atheist get insurance against acts of God? Why do they put braille on drive-through ATM's? Why do they lock gas station bathrooms? Are they afraid someone will clean them?

There are practical questions. What am I going to do with my life? Where should I go to college? Is this the right person to marry? How many kids do we want to have? Where do we want to raise them? Should I buy a Chevy or a Ford? Team Kobe, Lebron or Jordan? Pizza or burgers for dinner? Should we vacation at the beach or in the mountains?

There are spiritual questions. Why is there so much evil in the world? Do all religions lead to God? Is there any real truth? Is there only one way? Is there a heaven and hell? If there is a hell, how could a loving God send someone there? Why do I exist? How do we know the Bible is accurate?

Of course, we could go on and on.

Most questions in life have one common element which is illustrated by the following story. A college sophomore tried to prove how smart he was by asking his professor the following question, "Is the bird I'm holding dead or alive?" If the professor said the bird was dead, the boy was going to free the bird and let it fly away; if the professor said it was alive, the boy was going to suffocate the bird. The professor was a seasoned veteran when it came to dealing with college students so he looked at the young man and said, "The answer is in your hands."

What a powerful truth.

Word On the Street

Jesus performed many miracles. He fed the multitudes, healed the sick, cast out demons and raised the dead. Due to His immense popularity, pressure began to develop from the authorities. While they kept demanding a sign, He kept pointing to their sins.

Because of this, Jesus knew His time on earth was limited. So in Matthew 16 He takes the disciples to the District of Caesarea Philippi. It was a region roughly twenty-five miles northeast of the Sea of Galilee and 120 miles from Jerusalem. The region was strongly identified with various religions and had once been the center for idol worship. It was an area where the Greeks had built many shrines and Herod the Great had built a temple honoring Caesar Augustus.

The population of Caesarea Philippi was mainly non-Jewish. As a result there would not have been any crowds vying for Jesus' attention, nor would there have been any Jewish leaders looking to arrest Him. Caesarea Philippi was the perfect place for Jesus to bring the disciples for some much needed solitude.

As mentioned above, time was growing short. The cross was on the horizon and it was imperative they had a clear understanding of who Jesus was, why He had been born and what He came to do.

It was in this background that Jesus asked the most important question, “Who do people say the Son of Man is?” (Matthew 16:13) NIV

Jesus wants to know what the word on the street is. What are the people saying about me?

The disciples begin sharing what they had heard. “Some say John the Baptist; others say Elijah; and still others, Jeremiah or one of the prophets.” (Matthew 16:14) NIV

Why John the Baptist? Both preached the message, “Repent for the kingdom of heaven is at hand.”

Why Elijah? It had been prophesied that Elijah would come again. Both had a ministry of prayer, power and miracles. When Jesus and Elijah prayed, God answered.

What about Jeremiah? Jeremiah was known as the weeping prophet. He had a huge heart for the people and it was evidenced through his acts of compassion toward others. In the same way, Jesus was moved by compassion when it came to the needs of those around him.

One thing is for certain, we can never make a clear decision about who Jesus is by taking a poll of the people.

Popular Opinion

In 2011 Jesus was the most popular person in America behind Abraham Lincoln. He had a 90 percent approval rating.

All major religions believe Jesus was a prophet of God. Muslims say, "Prophet, yes. Messiah, no." Buddhists call Him a guru and an incarnation of Buddha. Mormons say, "He is a Son of God, along with many others." Philosophers acknowledge Jesus as one of the greatest teachers in history. Jews say, "Teacher, yes. Messiah, no." Liberals, atheists, and spiritualists of all types admit, "Impeccable man, yes. Divine, no." Historians point to Him as one of the most influential men who ever lived.

Most people are willing to admit Jesus was at least a prophet, activist, holy man, moral teacher, and spiritual leader. But when you speak of Jesus as the Messiah, Divine, or of the same nature as God, people will line up to express their disapproval.

A person can know many things about Jesus, but not know Him in the only way that matters. That is why Jesus turns the question away from the crowds to the disciples, "What about you?" he asked. "Who do you say I am?" (vs. 15)

This is the most important question a person will answer in life. A right confession of who Jesus is, is absolutely essential to our salvation.

If you declare with your mouth, "Jesus is Lord," and believe in your heart that God raised him from the dead, you will be saved. For it is with your heart that you believe and are justified, and it is with your mouth that you profess your faith and are saved. (Romans 10:9-10) NIV

So everyone who acknowledges me before men, I also will acknowledge before my Father who is in heaven, but whoever denies me before men, I also will deny before my Father who is in heaven. (Matthew 10:32-33) ESV

This is not a question; it is THE question.

Who do you say Jesus is?

Neutrality is not an option. Neither is avoiding the question.

No one on the planet was more qualified to answer this question than these men. They had been with Jesus day and night for three years. They heard Him teach, they saw His miracles and they felt His prayers. He shocked them. He thrilled them. He left them in awe and wonder.

In Matthew 8:27 they wondered aloud, "What kind of man is this?"

Now, the time had come for them to answer the most important question in life, "Who do YOU say I am?"

Jesus wasn't concerned about public opinion, He was concerned about their personal opinion.

Peter, being the strong one, steps to the front. He looks Jesus in the eye and makes the most incredible declaration, "You are the Christ, the Son of the Living God."

This is a monumental confession. There had been confessions before. The disciples declared Jesus to be the Son of God after He calmed the storms, but this time was different. This was not an emotional statement following a miracle. Peter is making a well calculated, sincere declaration of belief. Christ is the Greek form of the Hebrew word Messiah, which means Anointed One. Peter was declaring, "You are the One we have been waiting for. The Hope of Israel. Our Deliverer."

I imagine Jesus was filled with joy. His entire ministry led to this one confession and Peter had been paying attention. Jesus looks at him and says, "Blessed are you, Simon son of Jonah, for this was not revealed to you by flesh and blood, but by my Father in heaven." (Matthew 16:17) NIV

The confession is not the end of Peter's journey, but the beginning. With the proclamation came a responsibility.

"I tell you, you are Peter, and on this rock I will build my church, and the gates of hell shall not prevail against it. I will give you the keys of the kingdom of heaven, and whatever you bind on earth shall be bound in heaven, and whatever you loose on earth shall be loosed in heaven." (Matthew 16:18-19) ESV

Jesus says to Peter, "You are a rock, but you are only a small part of a larger structure. What you just confessed, 'I am the Christ, the Messiah, the Son of God,' will be the cornerstone, the foundation of a new organism called The Church."

Then Jesus says something strange, "He strictly charged the disciples to tell no one that he was the Christ." (vs. 20) ESV

Time out? The entire nation of Israel has been waiting centuries for you, and you don't want anyone to know? What's up with that Jesus? Isn't now the time to call the royal chariots, gather up the band, drop the banners, charge up the confetti machine and contact the local newspaper? It's time to throw the Jamma Jammy Jam of the Year. The Messiah is in the House! What are you going to do about this Rome? Where you at Caesar? Herod who? The Anointed One is here to deliver His people and there isn't anything you can do about it. Booyah! Mic Drop! I mean this is what I would do.

Good thing I'm not Jesus.

Jesus says, "You better not tell anyone. Peter, you understand this right?"

Peter, "But, but, but." "Nope, not a word," Jesus.

"From that time Jesus began to show his disciples that he must go to Jerusalem and suffer many things from the elders and chief priests and scribes, and be killed, and on the third day be raised." (vs. 21) ESV

Old News

For most of us this story is old news. If you have been a Christian for any period of time, you know the story of Good Friday and Easter. Even if you are not a Christian, you probably know the general outline. No matter what we believe about this story, it's not, "new news," to us. We've heard it before and therein lies the problem. It's hard to understand the shock of what Jesus is saying because we've heard it so many times. The disciples were hearing this for the very first time, so the thought of the Messiah being murdered would have staggered them.

In Mark's account, according to Peter, he adds that Jesus spoke "plainly" about the future. Meaning He didn't sugarcoat it. He didn't say, "Guys, I hate to break this to you, but we might encounter a few protesters in Jerusalem. Nothing big, just a few signs, and maybe a few people with megaphones and their chests painted in opposition. No worries though, God is with us."

No. Jesus said plainly, "I am going to be killed."

This created a problem for Peter because he had been expecting a different kind of Messiah. In his mind, the Messiah would come in strength and power. He would defeat the Roman occupation and lead Israel in a worldwide revolution. None of this made sense. Jesus had gone crazy. He's proclaimed, "Messiah," and all of the sudden it goes to His head.

Peter did what we generally do when we think someone we love is talking crazy. He pulled Jesus aside, "Excuse me Jesus. Have you lost your mind? What is wrong with you?"

Maybe he was trying to encourage Jesus. Maybe he meant to say, "I know people are after your life, but don't worry about it. There are twelve of us. They'll have to go through us to get to you."

Either way, you can't get around it. He "rebuked" Jesus.

Rebuke means to, "haul over the coals, scold, reprimand, give a talking to." Peter didn't dance around it. He said, "Jesus, I don't like what you are saying and you better stop it!"

Sit Down and Shut Up…Satan

Have you ever asked, "What was he thinking?" This is one of those moments. I'm no scholar, but I know enough to understand it wasn't a smart move for an aspiring apostle to rebuke the Son of God.

Jesus wasn't having it either. He looks at Peter again and says, "Get behind me, Satan! You are a hindrance to me. For you are not setting your mind on the things of God, but on the things of man." (vs. 23) ESV

Some of the harshest language Jesus ever spoke was when He was talking to Peter. Though He used more colorful language when He criticized the Pharisees, He never called them Satan. Even though the Bible says Satan entered Judas, Jesus never called him

Satan, either. Peter remains the only person Jesus ever called Satan. Quite the downgrade from the "Rock," isn't it?

What was Peter thinking?

Let's state the obvious:

First, he loved Jesus and wanted to spare Him the pain of this prophecy. Even if it might come true. This actually happens quite often. There have been many occasions where a friend or loved one is brought in for prayer. While one is being honest about their condition and knows unless God intervenes death is inevitable, the other one rebukes them and says, "Don't talk like that. Think Positive. You're gonna beat this." No one wants to hear someone they love talk about death. It's just the way it is, a natural coping mechanism. The first stage of grief is denial.

Second, Peter didn't understand God's plan. When Peter proclaimed Jesus as, "Christ, the Son of the living God," this is not what he had in mind. He never thought it would include the shame and horror of public crucifixion. He couldn't grasp how someone as good and holy and compassionate as Jesus would be forced to suffer and die like a common criminal. He couldn't see God's purpose in the pain. The Messiah was supposed to deliver them from the enemy's hands, not be delivered into the enemy's hands.

Third, he thought he knew God's will better than Jesus did. He didn't think Jesus knew what He was talking about. He thought he knew God's plan for Jesus better than Jesus knew God's plan for Jesus. This is why Peter's life is one big paradox. You can't call Jesus the Son of God and then think you know more than Him. That's conflicting, yet we do it all the time. For example, we confess Jesus as Lord of our life, but have never allowed Him to be Lord of our finances. We think we know how to manage our money better than Him. He may be anointed but He isn't an accountant.

Fourth, he wanted a kingdom without a cross. Who could blame him? I know it's hard for us to understand the true horror of the cross because we sport them proudly. We display them on our cars and in our churches. We place them in our homes and tattoo them across our hearts. We even buy the biggest, brightest and shiniest one we can to wear around our neck. No Jew would have ever done such a thing. For the Jews in the first century, the cross was the ultimate instrument of public torture. To them the cross represented a brutal, bloody, agonizing and shameful death. It was a sign of public disgrace and God's disapproval. It would be very similar to Americans displaying an electric chair in their home or wearing it on a piece of jewelry. Who in their right mind would ever do such a thing?

It's no wonder Peter didn't hold back when rebuking Jesus.

But Jesus didn't hold back either. In front of the other disciples He rebuked Peter and said, "Get behind me, Satan!"

The solid rock has become a stumbling block.

Why would Jesus use such strong language?

Jesus knew that Satan was behind Peter's well-meaning but misguided words. Satan's plan for Jesus avoided the cross because the death of Christ would make the life of Christ available to all.

Peter didn't understand this.

To Peter the cross was condemnation; to Jesus the cross meant salvation.

To Peter the cross meant Jesus had been defeated; to Jesus the cross meant Satan was defeated.

To Peter the cross meant death had won; to Jesus the cross meant victory was achieved.

To Peter the cross meant Jesus was lost forever; to Jesus the cross meant we could live forever.

To Peter the cross was a badge of shame; to Jesus it was a sign of love.

So great was the difference on their idea of the cross that Jesus had to say, "Get behind me, Satan! You are a hindrance to me. For you are not setting your mind on the things of God, but on the things of man." (vs. 23)

If you are not feeling a little uncomfortable yet, Jesus then says to the rest of the group, "If anyone would come after me, let him deny himself and take up his cross and follow me. For whoever would save his life will lose it, but whoever loses his life for my sake will find it." (vs. 24-25)

A little hard to hear, isn't it?

I love the concept of salvation, especially the kind that costs me nothing. I sin, Jesus saves. I deserve hell, Jesus gives heaven. Who doesn't like that?

Peter apparently liked it. He loved the idea of Jesus being the Messiah but when it came to costing him something, well, there's always a line we won't cross.

It's easy to be with Jesus as long as He is doing something for us, but the moment He requires something from us we're out.

We are for Jesus as long as He is for us.

We like the moment of salvation but not a lifetime of discipleship. When hard times hit and life doesn't seem to be working out the way want, we get disappointed in Jesus and our devotion goes out the window. This is why Jesus is brutally honest about what it means to be His disciple. He makes no bones about it - following Him will cost you something.

Why? Because it cost Him everything.

I Pledge Allegiance

Luke writes that Jesus was arrested on the Mount of Olives. As He is being led away, Peter follows from a distance. I have seen this happen way too many times. People are willing to follow Jesus, but only from a distance. They are with Him, but only from a safe distance just in case they are asked if they are, "with Him." Being close might cost us something. We don't mind being an associate, but we are hesitant to give Him our allegiance.

Luke goes on to say, "When some there had kindled a fire in the middle of the courtyard and had sat down together, Peter sat down with them." (Luke 22:55) NIV

Instead of standing with Jesus Peter sits down with the crowd. He left his job to be an associate of Jesus, but when it might cost him his life and when his allegiance is tested, he sits down with the multitude.

This is a great picture of the kind of Christian we see in today's society. We want God to provide for us, to protect us, to answer our prayers, but when it comes to standing with Him in front of the crowd, we would rather take our seat among the crowd.

Peter's allegiance is about to be tested.

Luke says, "A servant girl saw him seated there in the firelight. She looked closely at him and said, 'This man was with him.' But he denied it. 'Woman, I don't know him,' he said. A little later someone else saw him and said, 'You also are one of them.' 'Man, I am not!' Peter replied. About an hour later another asserted, 'Certainly this fellow was with him, for he is a Galilean.'" (vs. 56-59)

In other words, because of your ancestry, because of your association, by all appearances, you must be one of Jesus' followers.

Peter adamantly replies, "I don't know what you're talking about!" (vs. 60)

Imposter

You can look like you are with Christ, be surrounded with people who are with Christ, be from a family that is with Christ, and still not be with Christ.

Peter proves it.

Three times people say, "You are with Christ." Three times he denies it.

Peter, you were with Christ when He was transfigured on the mountain. You saw Him bring Lazarus back from the dead. For goodness sake, you walked on water and He saved you from drowning! Peter, He called you the rock, the gatekeeper of heaven. Why would you lie? Why would you say you are not with Him?

Maybe he wasn't lying. Maybe Peter was for Jesus as long as Jesus was doing things for Peter. As long as Peter got a little glory or a little attention he was for Jesus, but when life got tough, a line had to be drawn in the sand.

Peter was for Peter more than he was for Jesus, so he denies Him.

I was with Him when He was with me, but I am no longer with Him when He can no longer do anything for me.

That hurts.

Peter left it all to follow Jesus. He was the one the other disciples looked up to. Peter was, "the man," but that's the problem; he was just a man.

He failed Jesus when Jesus needed him most.

'Til Death Do Us Part

My wife and I have been together for over twenty years. I will never forget seeing her for the first time. She was hotter than a fire cracker on the Fourth of July.

Which just so happened to be when we met.

I lived outside the city limits and her friend lived just inside, so they would often come to my house to shoot off fireworks. The first time I met Amy she picked up a frog she thought was a fire cracker. It was a sign of things to come because she was about to turn this frog into a Prince.

The moment she said, "Come and see this," I was hooked. I had never met anyone so beautiful inside and out. Not sure if it was her jean shorts, the hot July evening, or the smell of frog urine, but something woke up a desire in me I had never experienced before. I knew she was the one for me. After a few tries she finally agreed to go on a date and I've been blessing her socks off ever since. Because she is more than enough, I cannot get enough. Thank you Jesus for breaking the mold when you made her!

We dated four years before we got married. Truth is, we never really had any tough times, but if we had, either one of us could have bailed at any time. I absolutely loved being with her, and I'm pretty sure she liked being with me, but we had no real allegiance to each other.

All of that changed on May 13, 2000, the day we got married! As we stood in front of our parents, peers, and the pastor, we made a commitment. We swore our allegiance to each other. In sickness and in health, for richer or for poorer, 'til death do us part, we will stay together, forever. We publicly pledged our love for one another. We are no longer together by association. We are together, even if there is a price to pay. When she hurts, I hurt. When she wins, I win. I am not just associated with her when times are good, I will stand with her even when times get bad.

If that wasn't enough, the pastor asked me to do something else. He asked me to wear a ring to signify to the world I am pledged to her. The ring didn't make me married, my vows did, but it did show the world I am now devoted to her.

Every morning I put on my ring to show my allegiance to Amy. I am not just an associate of Amy, I am committed to her. I am with her whether or not she is doing something for me and I stand with her even if it costs me.

Not Peter. He was sitting with the crowd when He should have been standing with Jesus.

All of a sudden, a rooster crows, and Peter remembers what Jesus said in Luke 22:34, "I tell you, Peter, before the rooster crows today, you will deny three times that you know me." NIV

Peter is devastated.

Don't Forget Peter

I believe either consciously or subconsciously, many of us are held hostage by past mistakes. It is difficult to get on our with lives because we can't get past our past. Mark Batterson says, "If you listen closely, you will hear many people define themselves by what they've done wrong, rather than defining themselves by what Christ did right." It is easier to define ourselves by the hurtful things done to us, than to define ourselves by the wonderful things Christ has done for us.

Do you have any regrets? Sure you do. Some are big, some are small. There's buyer's remorse and restaurant regret. There's the 80's clothing and the 90's hairdo. There's the accident that cost you your job and the mistake that cost you your marriage. Our regrets are as unique as we are.

The question is, "How do we deal with them?" Maybe a better question is, "Have you dealt with them?"

In Joshua 5, "The LORD said to Joshua, 'Today I have rolled away the shame of your slavery in Egypt.'" (vs. 9) NIV

Wait a minute. Israel walked out of Egypt forty years earlier.

They may have exercised their freedom but apparently they never exercised their demons. It wasn't until they reached Gilgal that they were able to leave their past in the past. That means it took forty long years and 381 miles to get the past out of their present.

Thankfully, Peter didn't have to wait that long.

As you know, Jesus was crucified. Praise the Lord, He didn't stay there. On the third day three women, Mary Magdalene, Mary the mother of James, and Salome went to the tomb.

But as they arrived, they looked up and saw that the stone, which was very large, had already been rolled aside. When they entered the tomb, they saw a young man clothed in a white robe sitting on the right side. The women were shocked, but the angel said, "Don't be alarmed. You are looking for Jesus of Nazareth, who was crucified. He isn't here! He is risen from the dead! Look, this is where they laid his body. Now go and tell his disciples, including Peter, that Jesus is going ahead of you to Galilee. You will see him there, just as he told you before he died." (Mark 16:4-7) NLT

Did you catch that? Including Peter.

The only name the angel mentions specifically is the guy who messed up significantly.

Any suffering Peter faced from this time on was well deserved. But the angel said, "Go tell the disciples, including Peter."

God was not through with him just yet.

Let that speak to all of you who have messed up so bad you think He can never use you again. Wherever you are at, today is not the end of your story.

John records Jesus appearing to the women, to the disciples, and Thomas. At the end of chapter 20 John wrote:

The disciples saw Jesus do many other miraculous signs in addition to the ones recorded in this book. But these are written so that you may continue to believe that Jesus is the Messiah, the Son of God, and that by believing in him you will have life by the power of his name. (John 20:30-31) NLT

This would be a great way to end his book. What more could He say? Jesus is alive, and He is walking around. There is proof He is who He said He was.

But God wouldn't let John finish just yet. One thing is still missing.

It is important to know Matthew wrote to the Jews. Mark wrote to the Gentiles. Luke wrote a history account. But John's gospel is personal.

He records more miracles and intimate details about Jesus than the others. He even records something about Peter no one else does. God would not allow his account to close until Peter's full story had been told.

At some point between Jesus' crucifixion, resurrection, and ascension, Peter decided to go back to his old life. He assumed his future had passed so he went back to what he knew best.

We know Peter had seen Jesus at least twice after His resurrection. In John's gospel, Peter is the first person to enter the empty tomb. In Luke's account, the women's report of the empty tomb is dismissed by the apostles, but Peter decides to check it out himself. In fact, he runs to the tomb. When he gets there he sees for himself, the tomb is empty!

Sometime after this, Peter went back to the place he was most comfortable. A fishing boat on the Sea of Galilee.

Going Fishing

I love to fish. I grew up fishing with my dad and brothers, so fishing reminds me of my childhood. Honestly, I don't think it's as much about fishing as it is the experience. Is there anything better than sitting in a boat with a few lines in the water and a few Pepsi's in the cooler? It's almost therapeutic, like a massage of the soul. It just feels right. Ladies, if you want your man to talk to you, take him fishing. He'll open up like a tackle box.

It shouldn't be a surprise that Peter went back to fishing. A bad day fishing is always better than a good day at work. Sometimes you fish all day and don't catch a thing, but you still got to go fishing.

There is nothing wrong with fishing.

Unless fishing represents something.

For Peter it was easier to go fishing than it was to deal with his failure. Instead of dealing with his sin he would rather sit in a boat on a lonely lake and suffer through the devastation of his decision. No one wants to let Jesus down, so it's a good thing we didn't. It is impossible to let God down because you were never holding Him up. You can't be a disappointment to Him because nothing takes Him by surprise. So while Peter was sitting on a boat, Jesus was standing on the shore. What is He doing there? You are about to find out.

At dawn Jesus was standing on the beach, but the disciples couldn't see who he was. He called out, "Fellows, have you caught any fish?" (John 21:4-5) NLT

I love what Jesus does. He knows they hadn't caught anything because He made the fish for heaven's sake.

What He is really asking them is, "Do you think you can go your own way, do your own thing, and be happy? Do you think you can go back to your old life and find purpose? You're not really looking for fish, you're looking for purpose, peace and forgiveness, and you won't find it sitting on a boat in the middle of a lake. You will come up empty every time."

He then responds in the complete opposite way I would have responded. I would have put a hole in their boat, watched them sink and rescued them at the last possible minute. That is, if I rescued them at all. I know you are more spiritual than me, but that's how I roll. Good thing I'm not Jesus.

"No," they replied. Then he said, "Throw out your net on the right-hand side of the boat, and you'll get some!" So they did, and they couldn't haul in the net because there were so many fish in it. (vs. 6)

Jesus is the kind of guy I like to fish with. He knows where the fish are biting, He doesn't mind cooking or cleaning and He even has the place settings and table ready. Jesus is a good fishing buddy. But Jesus wasn't there because He liked fish; He was there because He loved the fishermen.

When Peter recognizes it is Jesus, he jumps out of the boat and swims to shore. When he got to the shore, Jesus was cooking by a fire.

Don't miss the irony.

Peter had denied Jesus by a fire and now Jesus brings him back to a fire to reestablish him. This is just like Jesus. Instead of disciplining him in the middle of his disobedience in front of the other disciples, He calls him a friend and cooks him breakfast. This is the message of the Gospel. In the middle of our disobedience Jesus reaches out to us. He doesn't just reach out to us, He redeems and restores us.

Sometime after breakfast, Jesus reveals why He was really there. He needed to have a talk with Peter. Thankfully, John records their conversation. Jesus asks Peter three times, "Do you love me?" Peter responds each time, "Yes, Lord, you know I love you."

The English translation of their conversation misses the magnitude of the moment. The Koine Greek language is very precise. There are at least four different words for "love" in the Greek. Agape is sacrificial love, it is a love that keeps on loving even when the loved one is unresponsive, unkind, unlovable, and unworthy. It is an unconditional love. Phileo means a friendly love. This love speaks of affection, fondness or liking. The kind of love that exists among friends. Eros describes the love that exists between a man and a woman, a love full of passion. Storge is a quiet, abiding feeling within a person that rests on something close to him that he feels good about, much like a love that exists between master and pet.

The first two times Jesus asked Peter if he loves him, he asks, "Peter, do you agapao me?" Is your allegiance to me? Would you die for me? Peter says, "Yes, Lord you know I do."

The third time Jesus asks, "Peter, do you phileo me?" Do you love me by association?

Peter was hurt because he was being confronted with the truth. He replies, "Lord, you know everything. Yes, it is true, I love you by association, not by allegiance."

No matter what Peter wanted to believe, when it was time for Peter to publicly stand with Jesus, he was sitting with the crowd. When Jesus could no longer do anything for Peter, Peter would no longer do anything for Jesus.

Thankfully Jesus was not through with Peter. After each answer, Jesus recommissions Peter by saying, "Feed my sheep." It was His way of saying, "Don't give up on yourself Peter because God has not given up on you. In fact, your best days are still ahead."

The Rest of the Story

In Acts 2 the Festival of Pentecost is taking place. Jews had gathered from all around the world to worship in Jerusalem for the annual celebration of God's deliverance. In one of the most memorable moments in history, Peter stands before the crowd. Luke says he raises his voice, and for the next several moments he preaches with passion and power. His sermon pierced their hearts and at the conclusion they asked Peter what they had to do to be right with God.

Peter replied, "Repent and be baptized, every one of you, in the name of Jesus Christ for the forgiveness of your sins…Those who accepted his message were baptized, and about three thousand were added to their number that day." (Acts 2:38, 41) NIV

The guy who once sat with the crowd was now standing in front of the crowd declaring His allegiance to Jesus. From his sermon, the New Testament Church was born, sparking a revolution that would change the world!

There's a Little Bit of Peter in All of Us

Peter's life is one of contrasts. He is up, then he is down. He has faith, then he has fear. He speaks up, then remains silent. He is courageous, then he is a coward.

Peter is a conflicted soul. Much like you and I.

Proverbs says, "The godly may trip seven times, but they will get up again." (Proverbs 24:16) NIV

I am not sure there is a better verse to describe Peter's story. Yes, he failed, but each time he got back up. He did just as he told us to do. He grew in the grace of Jesus.

Never more is his growth most evident than in his writings.

Precious Promises

Peter wrote his letters toward the end of his life. At least five times over the course of his letters he uses a word I can't picture him using. It's the word "precious." I'm not sure about you, but when I think of the word precious, Peter doesn't come to mind. Peter was a rough and tough fishermen. I'm sure you've heard the phrase, "He cusses like a sailor." Well, a sailor is the cousin of a fisherman. Matthew tells us in chapter 26 of his gospel that Peter used swear words when denying Christ. In Acts 4, he is described as being uneducated, common and ignorant.

So when I hear the word, "precious," I don't automatically think of Peter; I think of my granny. Yet, he uses it five times. He describes, "his faith," as being precious. He describes, "the blood of Jesus," as precious. He describes Jesus as the precious, "living stone and cornerstone." He refers to, "the promises of God," as precious.

Life has a way of softening you and age has a way of bringing things into focus. As Peter grew in maturity, he realized the only thing that matters is Jesus and Jesus alone.

Peter's first letter was written to Christians who had been scattered over five parts of the Roman Empire due to persecution. They were suffering because of their identity as children of God. He was writing to encourage these new believers to stay true to their identity even though they were facing difficulties, something he hadn't done. Peter forgot his identity when it mattered most. He was supposed to be the rock, but instead he acted like sinking sand.

He didn't want them to make the same mistake.

Listen to how he describes them, "A chosen people, a royal priesthood, a holy nation, God's special possession…" (1 Peter 2:9) NIV

God chose them. He chose them because He loved them and if they would believe this, it didn't matter what everyone else thought.

He then says they are of royal birth. Can you imagine being of royal birth? If Prince William walks down my street and I shout, "William, you're a bum and a loser," do you think he cares? No, because he's royalty. He knows who He is.

Not only that, but they were also priests. This was massive for the Israelites because being born into the priestly line gave them huge status in their culture. Priests were granted access no one else had.

Peter says all of God's children have been given special access into His presence. We have been set apart by God as His own special possession.

Shouldn't these truths change our perspective? Of course they should.

When Victor Serebriakoff was fifteen, his teacher told him he would never finish school and that he should drop out and learn a trade. Victor took the advice and for the next seventeen years he was an itinerant doing a variety of odd jobs. He had been told he was a "dunce" and for seventeen years he acted like one. When he was thirty-two years old, an amazing transformation took place. An evaluation revealed that he was a genius with an IQ of 161. Guess what? He started acting like a genius.

Since that time, he has written books, secured a number of patents and has become a successful businessman. Perhaps the most significant event for the former dropout was his election as chairman of the International Mensa Society. The Mensa Society has only one membership qualification - an IQ of 140. So what made the difference in Victor's life? Did he all of a sudden get smart at the age of thirty-two? No. The only thing that changed was the way he saw himself.

Let's be honest, some of us need a new identity. Did you know the New Testament mentions a new identity in Christ more than 150 times? When you give your life to Jesus, He gives you a new identity. You are a new creation. Your past is just that, past.

Jesus paid the price and cast our sin as far as east is from the west never to be remembered any more. You may not have forgotten it, but He has. Peter understood this better than anyone. Thirty years later he wrote, "Love covers a multitude of sins." (1 Peter 4:8) NLT

Almost Forgot

One thing I left out. Jesus told Peter before the rooster crows you will deny me three times. Peter lived in the Galilean countryside and every morning he would hear the rooster crow. It is what they do after all. This could have been very detrimental to Peter. If he was not careful, the crow of the rooster would have reminded him of his sin every morning. It's hard to have a new identity when the first thing every morning you are reminded of your old one.

Why do roosters crow?

They crow to remind us a new day is here. With each new day comes a new opportunity to start over. Jeremiah wrote that with each new day comes a new set of mercies.

His mercies never end… they are new every morning. (Lamentations 3:22-23) CSB

The Hebrew word for new is Chadash, which means different, as in never before experienced.

The enemy wants to remind you every day of everything you have done wrong. God wants to remind you that with every day comes a new set of mercies. I think it's time you stop hearing the crow of condemnation and start hearing the crow of celebration. A new day is here and with it is a chance to start over.

There is now no condemnation for those who are in Christ Jesus. (Romans 8:1) NIV

If you have placed your faith in Jesus, the Bible says you are placed in Him, and if you are placed in Him, your sins have already been dealt with. He paid the price so you wouldn't have to. You are no longer defined by what you have done wrong but by what Christ has done right. Therefore, your sin is not your identity. So please don't give up on yourself because Christ has never given up on you.

If you need to go fishing to clear your head, go ahead and do it. Just know Jesus is waiting for you on the shore. Why? Because you are His friend. Your set back, is a set-up, for your comeback.

Sermon in a sentence: Don't give up on Jesus because He will never give up on you.

IN CHAINS BUT NOT ENCHAINED

CHAPTER 11
THE STORY OF PAUL

In 1985, a group of scientists decided to build an eight story, 3.14 acre glass and steal dome. The dome was meant to protect them from the outside elements but still allow them to live a full and complete life. The dome included a rainforest, ocean and coral reef, wetland, savannah grassland, fog desert and a complete agricultural system. It also included a human habitat that provided living quarters and office space. To make the structure as comfortable as possible the engineers included heat and air, hot and cold water and natural gas energy. The building housed everything needed to survive in order to be unaided by the outside world. Finally in 1991, eight people entered the facility known as the *Biosphere*, just outside Tucson, Arizona. No matter what happened on the outside, they would be unaffected on the inside. They planted their own seeds, grew their own food, and the outside world watched with a sense of jealousy. Let the rains come, the winds blow and the sun blaze. Nothing that happened on the outside could affect those on the inside.

Who hasn't longed for that sense of peace and security? Who hasn't longed to get away from it all? The world we live in is not the same as it once was. Our money is not a sure thing, jobs are not as secure as they once were and schools are not a safe place to send our children anymore. Turn on the evening news and discover more people are being mistreated, murder and suicide are at an all-time high, women are abused in the workplace and racism is still alive. Government leaders are in one scandal after another, children are neglected, church leaders are corrupt. Too much sun causes cancer, the air we breathe is full of toxins, the vegetables we eat cause sickness, the meat we buy contains too many chemicals and the water we drink is full of cancer causing poison. If you weren't worried when you started reading this chapter you are now, right?

We go to sleep worried and wake up worrying we didn't get enough sleep.

Two mothers of teenagers were talking and one said, "I'm worried, my daughter doesn't tell me anything." The other said, "I'm worried, my daughter tells me everything."

How can we find confidence when our world is so full of conflict? Wouldn't it be great to enter a biosphere, free from the worries of life?

Joy on the Journey When the Journey Is Not So Joyful

The Book of Philippians is often referred to as the Book of Joy. Paul uses some form of the word, "joy," sixteen times in his little letter to the church of Philippi. What is interesting about this book is that it is one of the four prison epistles of Paul, meaning Paul wrote it while in prison or under house arrest. How could he find joy when his journey was not so joyful?

By his own account he had lived a horrendous life, at least after he became a Christian he did. He had been imprisoned frequently, flogged severely and left for death on more than one occasion. He received thirty-nine lashes five different times, three times he was beaten with rods, once he was pelted with stones and three times he was shipwrecked. He had been robbed, mocked and stripped naked. He was constantly on the move due to threats on his life and he faced danger whether he was in the city or in the country. Believers and nonbelievers tried to kill him, but through it all, Paul was able to keep his joy. As he is sitting in prison awaiting trial for a crime he didn't commit, he encourages believers to rejoice in all things.

How is this possible?

Listen to what he says, "I am in chains for Christ… And because of this I rejoice…Yes, and I will continue to rejoice…" (Philippians 1:13, 18) NIV

Paul understood something most of us don't. Even though he was in chains, he still had the choice whether or not to be enchained. This is so important. I know you are facing situations you would not choose. No one chooses their chains but we all have them. Some feel chained to a sickness, others to shame. Some feel chained to a fear, others to a past failure. Some are chained to depression, others to a divorce. Some are chained to an addiction, others to an occupation.

Paul says that even though I have chains, my chains do not have me. No matter what happens to me, I still have the power to choose what I do with these chains.

In verse 18, he makes the most powerful statement, "What does it matter?"

Honestly, what does it matter? Most of our fears and worries don't matter.

Worry is one of the greatest thieves of joy. Worry comes from the Greek word, "anxious," which means to be pulled in two directions. Our hopes pull us in one direction and our fears pull us in another.

As a result, we are pulled apart.

The English translation of the word worry means to "strangle."

You know worry certainly does that.

Jesus summarizes His opinion of worry with two words: Irrelevant and irreverent. He said, "Who of you by being worried can add a single hour to his life?" (Matthew 6:27) NIV

Worry is irrelevant. It changes nothing. When was the last time you worried your way out of a problem? Imagine saying, "I got behind on my bills so I worried my way out of it. Guess what? It worked! I yelled at my kids, took some pills, lost a few nights sleep, and boom, every one of my worries went away!" It doesn't happen that way. Worry changes nothing but your blood pressure. All it does is give you heartburn, headaches and sleepless nights.

I read 40% of the things we worry about never happen, 30% regard the past, (which cannot be changed), 12% are focused upon the opinions of others, (which we can do nothing about), and 10% of our worries are about personal health, (which only worsens the problem). That means only 8% of the things we worry about are things we can actually do something about.

In other words, 92% of our worries are useless. It is irrelevant.

Worry is also irreverent. It is trying to take care of the problem ourselves because we don't believe God can, or will, take care of us. Worrying is believing God will not provide for and protect His children.

Worry is unconscious blasphemy.

This is why Paul is so adamant about not worrying for anything. Rick Warren says, "Manage your problems yes, but do not let your problems manage you."

Make a Choice and Make Sure It's a Good One

Along with the gift of perspective, one of the greatest gifts God gives His children is the ability to make a choice. I didn't choose the family I was born into. I didn't choose my upbringing. I didn't choose my handicaps. I didn't choose this pain. I may not be in control of my chains, but I am in control of my choices, and I choose how I view these chains.

Paul made the choice to rejoice because that was the one thing he could control. If you want to have joy on the journey, no matter what happens along the journey, you need to make certain choices.

In chapter four of Philippians Paul encourages us to make several choices.

1. Choose to Praise

Rejoice in the Lord always. I will say it again: Rejoice! (Philippians 4:4) NIV

Paul had persecution on the outside and problems on the inside, but whatever the circumstance, whatever the problem, he made the choice to rejoice. He may not be able to choose his chains, but he could choose how he viewed them and what he did with them.

One of the greatest freedoms man holds is the power of choice. Paul knew this. He took the power out of the enemy's hands by acknowledging that in every situation he still has the choice to rejoice.

He is so emphatic about the choice to rejoice that he states it twice. Why? Because it is easier to remember to eat your vegetables than it is to make the choice to rejoice. It is easier to remember everything that everyone ever said about you than it is to rejoice. It is easier to recall every link that made your chains or every pain that put you in prison than it is to rejoice.

But Paul, you don't know what I'm going through. Do you have your head so far up in the clouds that you've lost touch with the real world? Do you really think praise will get me out of my prison?

Let me remind you Paul is writing to the church of Philippi.

Paul first went to Philippi in Acts 16. He wanted to go to Asia, but the Holy Spirit sent him to Philippi instead. When he got there he met a business woman name Lydia. Sometime after their initial meeting, Lydia and her entire household were baptized. Things were looking good, but as you know, it's not far from the mountain top to the valley floor. Shortly after, a demon possessed girl began to heckle Paul. Paul got so annoyed by her that one day he rebukes the demon right out of her. You would think the people would be happy, but instead they were furious. The girl was a side show carny fortune teller who made them a ton of money and now their money maker was healed. They caused an uproar in the city and had Paul beaten and imprisoned.

It was in the Philippian prison where Paul discovered something that changed the rest of his life.

This is so important. You might want to get your pen and highlighter ready.

His feet may have been in chains, but his mouth was still free to praise.

He makes the choice to rejoice.

Not because he was on vacation. Not because he got a new car. Not because his job was going well and his likes were up. Not because Kiki loved him. Not because Resha was riding with him. Not because Shawty promised to never ever leave him. Not because his circumstances were releasing feel good endorphins. Not because he was self-medicating and vaping his pain away. No, at the midnight hour, in the darkest moment of his life, he said, "I didn't choose this prison, but I can choose to praise in this prison. I didn't choose this pain, but I choose to praise in this pain. I choose to praise in this jail even if it feels like hell."

All of the sudden the earth started shaking, the room started rattling, and the chains started breaking. That's what praise does. It takes us out of our prison and puts in the very presence of God. Pastor Steven Furtick calls it a "perspective shift."

Praise shifts our perspective from how big our problems are to how big our God is.

When we stop worrying and start worshiping, chains come off, doors open, habits break, spirits are lifted, peace is imparted, addictions are abolished and lives are changed.

The jailer came in and said, "I want to know a God who can give me a song in the night. I want a God who can give me praise in prison. I want a God who can loosen my chains. Money can't. Status can't. Power can't. But apparently whatever you have, can."

At that very hour, the jailor and his entire household were baptized.

When God's people send praise up, His presence comes down. When His presence comes down, His power goes out. When His power goes out, people show up!

Praise will break your chains or your chains will break your praise.

Scholars don't know what prison Paul was in when he wrote this, but I can tell you what prison he wasn't in: the prison of resentment. There is no prison like the prison of resentment.

Some of you are in the prison of resentment and it is making you bitter. If you don't break out of this prison, you are going to destroy every relationship you have.

The choice is yours. You can say to yourself, it wasn't right that I didn't have a good dad; it wasn't cool that I didn't get a good education; or I would be so much further along if I had supportive people around me. You can make that choice and continue to be bitter, or you can say, "I didn't choose these chains, but I can choose what I do with them. I am making the choice to rejoice."

I recently read of a study that showed music is one of the only things that mentally takes you above your circumstance while you are still physically in it.

Music is powerful. It was created by God to bring Him glory but also to do us good. It is one of the only things that ties our entire being together as it engages the mind, emotion, soul and body.

When combined with a sincere heart of worship, music is the most powerful expression a human being is capable of. To fail at worshiping God is the greatest failure a human can commit. It has the gravest and most immediate consequences. When you see a person that does not know how to worship, I will show you a person who is unhappy or dying on the inside.

The Bible says God inhabits the praise of His people. When a person worships Him in spirit and truth, He can't wait to show up and show off and do great miracles for that person. Who can blame Him?

When you go through intense times of pressure and can't feel the presence of God though the Bible or prayer, try singing. Try rejoicing. Take out a pen and paper and write down as many blessings as you can and praise Him. Praise ushers us into the very presence of God and lifts us out of life's prisons. Praise breaks loose the chains that hold us captive and provides light in the midst of darkness.

If you will learn to give yourself fully to God in worship, He will release you from any prison, any funk, any depression, any worry, any sickness, or any conflict you are in.

Don't worry, worship. Worship until the chains fall off and the doors start to open. If God has a weak spot, it's the praise of His people; He can't help but act.

2. Choose to Pray

Do not be anxious about anything, but in every situation, by prayer and petition, with thanksgiving, present your requests to God. And the peace of God, which transcends all understanding, will guard your hearts and your minds in Christ Jesus. (Philippians 4:6-7) NIV

If you want a worry free mind and a joy filled heart, then you need a fortified mind and secure heart.

Philippi was a garrison town for the Roman army. Soldiers were stationed on the outside of Philippi and freely walked the streets on the inside. Naturally, the citizens of Philippi felt safe. Paul says, "You see those troops Caesar sent to watch over your city? I have something better. When we send our prayers up, God sends His army down to stand guard over our hearts and minds."

When we worry, we are trying to secure ourselves, but when we pray and thank Him in advance, we are transferring our trust to Him. When we transfer our trust to Him, He sends them. Who is them? The Peace Team. The Peace Team surrounds me, guards me, protects me and comforts me. I don't always understand it, nor can I see it, but that doesn't keep me from experiencing it. The chains are still here, but because I made the choice to rejoice and the choice to pray, God's peace protects me. Even in the midst of this jail I can still have joy, because God has given me Jesus and Jesus is all I need.

Notice Paul said, "Rejoice in the Lord… and have peace in Jesus." (vs. 4, 7)

As long as I have Jesus, I have peace; but if I don't have Jesus, all I have are a bunch of pieces.

This is why prayer is so important.

The disciples had heard Jesus preach the greatest sermons ever. They had seen Him heal the sick, raise the dead and bend molecules by turning water into wine. They saw a man who had been lame for thirty-eight years develop calf muscles and start walking. Yet they didn't ask, "Lord, teach us to speak like you, heal like you, and raise the dead like you." Instead they asked, "Lord, teach us to pray like you."

They understood prayer was the key to the power in Jesus' life.

While sitting in a jail cell in Philippi, Paul praised and prayed. You need the one-two punch of prayer and praise in your life. There is nothing more powerful and more important in your life than this combo. God will show up to receive our praise, but if you want to see an outpouring of God's presence in your life then you need to understand the power of prayer.

Prayer and praise promise to bring God's presence into every situation.

For many people, when they think of prayer, one word comes to mind: boring. That's not the type of prayer meetings we see happening in the Bible. When God's people prayed, exciting things happened.

When they had prayed, the place in which they were gathered together was shaken… (Acts 4:31) ESV

That doesn't sound boring to me. That sounds exciting.

After Moses came down from Mt. Sinai, praying became an earmark of Israel's success and in his farewell speech he made sure he mentioned this.

What other nation is so great as to have their gods near them the way the Lord our God is near us whenever we pray to him? (Deuteronomy 4:7) NIV

Other nations may have had better chariots and weapons but that didn't matter. They didn't have what Israel had: a God who would fight for His people when called upon.

David said, "You can be sure of this…The LORD will answer when I call to him." (Psalm 4:3) NLT

I can hear David saying, "You can chase me, beat me, mock me, do whatever you want, but beware, when I call on God, you're in trouble."

He also said, "Because he bends down to listen, I will pray as long as I have breath!" (Psalm 116:2) NLT

As long as David had breath in him, he was going to pray.

One of the chief characteristics of God's people has always been that they are a praying people. In fact, Psalm 14:4 describes the wicked as people, "who have never learned to call upon the LORD."

Jesus did not say His house shall be called a house of teaching, a house of music or house of reading God's Word. They are important, however, they must never override prayer as the defining mark of God's presence. Revelation 8:4 describes prayer as "incense that rises up before God day and night." Something wonderful happens within in the heart of God when His children put themselves out on a limb and say from the depths of their soul, "I can't fix this. It is beyond me. I need you. All my eggs are in your basket and I am staying here until you act on my behalf."

Sadly, most Christians have never prayed that way, or heard anyone else pray with such urgency.

As I look back over my life, I can see every step forward has been accomplished through the power of prayer.

I believe we would see God move much more in our life and experience His presence more fully if we would just take Him more seriously by praying. I'm not talking about a quick supper time prayer. I'm talking about a faith filled prayer the Bible describes as crying out, lifting up our voice and begging God to act on our behalf.

James says, "The fervent prayer of a righteous man results in much." (James 5:16) KJV

Fervent means passionate, intense, enthusiastic, fanatical, wholehearted, eager and committed. James says that is the kind of prayer God answers, the fervent ones. The ones that say I am not letting go or giving up until I receive a blessing from the hand of

God. If I have to stay here all night, I will. If I have to knock until my knuckles get raw, I will. If I have to ask until my voice goes out, I will. If I have to cry until my tears are gone, I will. Jesus taught us to keep on asking, keep on seeking and keep on knocking. For everyone who asks, receives. He who seeks, finds and He who knocks, the door will be opened.

Don't believe me? Ask Paul.

His feet were in chains but his mouth was still free to pray and praise.

What happened? The prison doors flew open.

The truth is, we see God move so little in our lives because we expect so little from Him. Jesus said, "It shall be done according to our faith." When you believe God can, that's a fact. When you believe He might, that's hope. When you believe He will, that's faith.

"I tell you the truth, anyone who believes in me will do the same works I have done, and even greater works, because I am going to be with the Father. You can ask for anything in my name, and I will do it, so that the Son can bring glory to the Father. Yes, ask me for anything in my name, and I will do it!" (John 14:12-14) NLT

This is the most amazing verse. Jesus says we shall do greater works than He did. How is that possible? Through prayer. Jesus voluntarily limited Himself by becoming human. He could only be in one place at one time and He could only do miracles where He was at. But prayer is not limited by time or space. I can pray for my family in Oklahoma while I am in Arizona. And the prayers I pray today may be answered today, tomorrow, one year or one decade from now.

Every Saturday night for six years I prayed over every seat in the sanctuary of the church I pastored. I memorized where everyone sat so I would be able to pray for each person by name. I begged for God to touch their souls. I begged God for our church to experience His presence. I begged for our church to grow. I prayed so hard I would often lose my voice. During my six years as Pastor of that church I developed stomach ulcers. As weird as it sounds, I believe part of the reason I developed those ulcers was from praying so hard because I wanted our church to experience revival so bad.

God had other plans.

At the time of this writing, I have been the Lead Pastor of Mountain View Church over six years. In the past six years we have baptized close to 1,500 people and seen over 2,000 give their lives to Christ. Everything I prayed so hard for, so many years ago, is taking place here every Sunday. I thought my prayers were not being answered, but what I didn't know was, I was sending them on ahead. The harvest we are experiencing now is because of the seeds sowed many years ago.

God can do more than you ever imagine and He often chooses to do it through our prayers. He can take you out of a dead end job and put you in the corner office. He can give you favor when it looks like you have failed. He can rekindle the flame in your marriage when the spark went out years ago. He can change a heart, heal a soul and break an addiction. He can look at any situation that seems like it has been dead for days or decades, hopeless and beyond repair, and bring it back to life. With God, a delay is not a denial. A knock down is not a knock out. Failure is not final. If you believe this, then start praying like you do, and you will see even greater works than these.

If you really want to worry less, pray more.

A person once asked his friend, "How are you doing?" His friend was upset about something that had happened so he replied,

"I'm doing alright under the circumstances." His friend replied, "What are you doing under the circumstance?"

God doesn't want us to be under any circumstance. God wants us to be overcomers and the way we become overcomers is through the power of prayer.

In 1937 architect Frank Lloyd Wright built a house for industrialist Hibbard Johnson. One rainy evening, Johnson was entertaining a few distinguished guests when the roof began to leak. The water seeped through directly above where Johnson was sitting, dripping steadily onto his head. Irate, he called Wright and said, "Frank, you built this beautiful home and we enjoy it very much. But the roof leaks and right now I am with friends and honored guests and it is leaking on my head." There was a pause on the other end of the line. Finally, Frank replied, "Well Hib, why don't you move your chair."

Prayer is moving the chair. It is getting out from under the circumstance, taking control of the circumstance and making the choice to rejoice!

3. Choose the Right Focus

Finally, brothers and sisters, whatever is true, whatever is noble, whatever is right, whatever is pure, whatever is lovely, whatever is admirable—if anything is excellent or praiseworthy—think about such things. (Philippians 4:8) NIV

We can't choose our chains but we can choose what we focus on. I can focus on my chains or I can focus on God working through my chains. What you focus on is what you end up feeling. Think about lovely things and life will be lovely. Think about pure things and you will be pure. Think about praise worthy things and you will see God is worthy of your praise.

We need to think about what we are thinking about.

Paul saw that despite his chains the Gospel was advancing and good things were happening despite his circumstance. I think if you focus hard enough, you will see the same is true for you.

4. Choose To Be Content

I have learned to be content whatever the circumstances. I know what it is to be in need, and I know what it is to have plenty. I have learned the secret of being content in any and every situation, whether well fed or hungry, whether living in plenty or in want. (Philippians 4:11-12) NIV

Paul wasn't born content. He had to learn it through the school of hard knocks, the school of shipwrecks, stonings and shackles. However, He learned through it all that his situation does not have to regulate his satisfaction. Contentment is not a disposition, but a decision to make the choice to rejoice in all things. Whether you have a lot, or have a little, you can be content. Paul had to learn this lesson the hard way.

5. Choose the "Can Do" Spirit

I can do all this through Him who gives me strength. (Philippians 4:13) NIV

The key phrase in Paul's most famous verse, is the phrase "through Him." I don't have joy, but He does. I don't have the confidence, but He does. I don't have the strength, but He does. I don't have the provisions, but He does.

I will not be moved by what I see, I'm moved by what I know. Through Him I can do all things!

Beat this addiction, yes. Have a better marriage, yes. Get a better job, yes. Start that new business, yes. Give my kids a better life, yes. Overcome temptation, yes. Be joyful again, yes. Accomplish my dreams, yes.

I can do all things… not some things… all things… not a few things… all things… What can I do? All things through Christ.

Through Him I can be healed. Through Him I can be promoted. My connection with Christ makes all the difference. This is a rock-solid certainty that no matter what happens to me, I can have peace, I can have hope, I can have joy and I can have confidence while feeling conflicted. From this moment on I'm gonna stop considering my chains and start considering Christ because through Him I can do all things!

I choose to believe it and I choose to accept it.

6. Choose to Believe It

And my God will meet all your needs according to the riches of his glory in Christ Jesus. (Philippians 4:19) NIV

Paul makes it personal. He says, "My God…will meet all of your needs…"

David said the same thing in Psalm 23, "The Lord is My shepherd…I shall not be in need."

What a difference one little word makes. It may be easy to believe in a God, it may even be easy to believe in an Intelligent Designer, but what matters most is if you believe this God cares about you and have made Him your Savior and shepherd. This is where it starts, by having a personal relationship with Jesus. This is the question we all have to answer, or at least wrestle with.

Is the Lord your shepherd?

If we get our relationship right with Him, then He will fulfill His responsibility to us.

In other words, if we make the Lord our shepherd, He will give us all we need.

So in the middle of the conflict in David and Paul's life, they looked up and said, "Why am I so afraid? Why am I so anxious? Why do I worry about my needs being met? Why do I get nervous at the end of the month? Why do I fret every time I get called into the office or come home from work? Why do I need man's approval so much?"

If God is my shepherd, that's all I need. If God is my shepherd, I will be okay. If God is my shepherd, I know I will be restored. If God is my shepherd, I will be blessed. If God is my shepherd, I will be anointed in the presence of my enemies. If God is my shepherd, I will be comforted. If God is my shepherd I know I will be okay. A good shepherd loves his sheep. A good shepherd provides for his sheep. And a good shepherd lays down his life for his sheep.

Not only will God meet all of my needs, He will meet all of your needs too. For a good shepherd there is no greater reward and no deeper satisfaction than that of seeing his sheep well fed, safe, flourishing and at peace in his care.

Paul says, "I know from personal experience, 'My God, shall meet all of your needs…in Christ Jesus.'"

The key phrase is, "in Jesus."

Jesus is where our needs are met, our strength is found, our confidence lies and our joy is found. All of our needs are met in Jesus!

So do whatever you have to do to get to Jesus. If you have chains that need breaking… get to Jesus. If you have a sickness that needs healing… get to Jesus. If you have a relationship that needs mending… get to Jesus. If you have a sin that needs forgiving… get to Jesus. If you have a child that needs saving… get to Jesus. Whatever you need, Jesus has it, so just get to Him. Whether you run, walk, crawl, roll, or inch your way to Jesus, just get to Jesus!

Apart from Him we have nothing, but in Him and through Him, we have everything we will ever need.

I have no idea what situation you find yourself in, but God has you right where He wants you. Even if it's not where you want to be, it's where you need to be. So don't look for the exit, look for Jesus.

There is power in the name of Jesus to break every chain.

Biosphere Flop

After twenty-four months the biosphere proved to be a total disaster. Oxygen levels dipped too low, ants conquered most of the other bugs, the experiments failed, the researchers couldn't get along and the dome was abandoned.

Nothing on this earth is secure.

Nothing can protect you like Jesus can.

The dome of His protection still stands.

We may not be in control of our situation, but we are in control of our choices, and we always get to choose how we respond to our chains.

Paul says, "I can do all things through Christ who gives me strength."

This includes making the choice to be confident, even though I feel conflicted.

What's that sound I hear? It could be your chains breaking free.

Sermon in a Sentence: Praise will break your chains or your chains will break your praise.

CONCLUSION
"BUT GOD"

In the introduction, I stated that every belief, every blessing, every promise, every prayer has a "but" attached to it. No matter how hard we try, it's hard to kick the "buts." Most of us have learned to hide them, but those who know us best have seen them. They know our "buts" better than we do.

Of course you know by now the "but" I am referring to represents our inner conflict. It is the tension between the faith we have and the frustrations we feel. As you have seen throughout this book, we are not alone in this conflict.

Paul is humble enough to even write about his own.

"I do not understand what I do. For what I want to do I do not do, but what I hate I do…As it is, it is no longer I myself who does it, but it is sin living in me. For I have the desire to do what is good, but I cannot carry it out. For I do not do the good I want to do, but the evil I do not want to do—this I keep on doing. Now if I do what I do not want to do, it is no longer I who do it, but it is sin living in me that does it. So I find this law at work: Although I want to do good, evil is right there with me. For in my inner being I delight in God's law; but I see another law at work in me, waging war against the law of my mind and making me a prisoner of the law of sin at work within me. What a wretched man I am!" (Romans 7:15-24) NIV

No wonder Paul says wretched. He has a lot of "buts."

So do I. So do you.

So what now?

Not One Direction, Every Direction

Paul wrote to the church of Corinth, "When we arrived in Macedonia, there was no rest for us. We faced conflict from every direction, with battles on the outside and fear on the inside." (2 Corinthians 7:5) NLT

No matter where Paul travels he cannot find rest or remove his conflict. He goes from one worry to another. One problem gets fixed, another arises. One bill gets paid, two more come up. Battles on the outside, fear on the inside. I didn't expect that. I didn't see that coming. I'm afraid of what might happen. I'm worried how this is gonna turn out. I have faith but I am frustrated and it's discouraging.

All of a sudden, Paul turns the situation around by using two little words, "But God." (vs. 6)

Those two words change everything.

"But God remembered Noah." (Genesis 8:1) NLT

"You intended to harm me, but God intended it for good." (Genesis 50:20) NLT

"My flesh and my heart may fail, but God is the strength of my heart and my portion forever." (Psalm 73:26) NIV

"You killed the author of life, but God raised Him from the dead." (Acts 3:15) NIV

"But God demonstrates his own love for us in this: While we were still sinners, Christ died for us." (Romans 5:8) NIV

Your situation may feel hopeless, but God. You may be sick, but God. You may be depressed, but God. You may be broke, but

God. You may be single, but God. You may be divorced, but God. You may feel conflicted, but God.

Those two words stand in direct opposition to the negative voices of this world. The world may say you can't, "But God," says you can. The world says you won't, "But God," says you will. The world says defeat, "But God," says victory!

Why is it easier to say, "But I," than it is to say, "But God?"

I need to work out… "But I" don't have the time.

I need to stop yelling at my kids… "But I" am so frustrated at the way they act.

I need to address the issue… "But I" don't like confrontation.

I need to quit… "But I" don't have what it takes.

I need to get a new job… "But I" am not qualified.

I need to change… "But I" don't like change.

I need to give… "But I" am broke.

You need to replace your ,"But I," with a, "But God."

The doctor says disease, "But God," says healing!

The world says hate, "But God," says love!

The world says destruction, "But God," says restoration!

The enemy says that you're finished, you're too old, you're washed up, "But God" says, 'I'm just getting started."'

Humanly speaking, some things are impossible, but with God all things are possible. All you have to do is add the two words, "But

God." Every time I read a verse in the Bible that says, "But God," good news follows.

If you are hurting and have challenges at home or in your health, or have conflict at work or with your wealth, my prayer as you conclude this book is that you know without a shadow of doubt there is a God who is for you.

So stop saying, "But I," and start saying, "But God!"

I believe someone reading this needs this.

You may have picked up this book because you are discouraged. You may even be saying to yourself, "I am not going to make it, I can't get this done, I will never get through this, my kids are going to continue going the wrong way, I'm always going to struggle financially, my health is going to get worse, I may never have a good marriage, and I will always have trouble on the outside and fear on the inside."

I want you to know that is not true. You can get better, you can have a great marriage, you can defeat temptation, you can be made whole, and your dreams will come to pass. You just need to fight that fear with faith.

I know you want to believe this badly, but there is voice inside of you that is suspicious, even after reading this book.

Whichever voice you feed, grows. Whichever one you starve, dies.

Why not feed the voice of faith today? You've fed the voice of doubt and insecurity for too long. It's time to raise our expectations, shake off our self-pity, get rid of our negativity, delete our disappointments, eliminate our fears, repent of our sinfulness and say, "God, I'm ready for a breakthrough!"

Jesus asked two blind men in Mathew 9:28, "Do you believe that I am able to do this?" Why would He ask this? The next verse tells us, "According to your faith, it shall be done." (vs. 29)

There is a direct connection between our faith and God's favor.

Look Up

In the middle of one the most obscure Old Testament books, Habakkuk is trying to reconcile what he believes in his heart with what he sees with his eyes. Life had not turned out the way he thought it would and he is conflicted. In the last verse of chapter two he says, "But the LORD… is in his holy temple."

When he looks up he makes an astounding observation. The Lord is still on His throne and because the Lord is still on His throne, it doesn't matter what we are going through, what diagnosis we have been given, or how conflicted we are. But the Lord is still in control. But the Lord is still mighty. But the Lord is still powerful. But the Lord is still able. I know it's almost 2019, "But the Lord," is the same, yesterday, today and forever!

Because the Lord is still on His throne, no matter what is happening around us, even when it doesn't make sense, and the clouds of doubt roll in, the righteous will not live by what they see; they will live with confidence knowing the best is yet to be.

To get out of your hell, you need hope to see what others can't see and believe God is not finished with you yet. Your dream may be deferred but that does not mean it is denied.

Please don't lose hope. He who began a good work in you will carry it through until the day of completion. I encourage you to live with a holy anticipation, always looking for the hand of God.

You see what you seek.

So anticipate great things, believe in better things, keep hope alive!

You need faith and hope.

Faith believes God can but hope gives us the excitement He will.

"But the LORD….is in his holy Temple."

Temporary Tents

Do you believe God still does what He once did? I believe He does. When I put faith in Him and His ability to do the miraculous I am putting His name on the line, not mine.

Why not believe for more? God is not intimidated by more; He made His people for more.

In Genesis 38 a woman named Tamar is pregnant with twins. When she was ready to give birth, one of the baby's arms came out first. The midwife tied a scarlet cord around his arm planning to gently pull him out. Before she could, the baby pulled his arm back into the womb and his brother broke through the womb and was born first. She named him Perez, which means, breaking out.

One boy stretched to his purpose while the other settled into the safety of his mother's womb.

Every one of us is pregnant with potential, with purpose, with possibility.

Within us is a stretcher and settler. One says, "I will become everything God has created me to be because I am made for more, so more is what I'm after."

The other one says, "I like where I am at. It may not be what I want, but it's good enough. My marriage is not great, but it's good enough. My health is not perfect, but it's good enough. I don't have the job I want, but it's good enough."

One wants to stretch and one wants to settle.

Too many people make the choice to settle for good enough. This book is about helping you see good enough is not your destiny. You are a child of the Most High God, therefore seeds of possibility have been placed within you. God breathed life into you and when He did it, He deposited Himself into you. You have a supernatural DNA within your natural DNA.

The first commandment God gave to His children was to go forth and multiply, to increase, to bear fruit, to make room for more. God set up a precedent that His children were not made to reach one level and settle. We were made to stretch into new territories, new rivers, and new lands.

But as you know, life has a way of getting us to "settle" where we are.

In Genesis 11, Abraham's father Terah left Ur. He set out towards Canaan, but when he reached Harran, he settled there. The last verse of chapter 11 says that he died there.

Harran was not where he was supposed to die. He was supposed to die in Canaan but the journey was long, difficult and discouraging, so he decided to stop and settle in Harran.

He knew it wasn't the Promised Land, but the pressure was too great, the problems too many and the pain too unbearable. He decided Harran was good enough. He didn't want to stretch because he was just trying to survive, so he settled halfway to his destination.

How many times have we done the same thing? We start pursuing our dream, we step into our destiny, but along the way opposition arises and adversity comes. Before long we begin to say, "Things are pretty good here, at least good enough, so I'll just stop and settle here a while."

We end up building a permanent dwelling when we were supposed to be putting up a temporary tent.

Temporary provisions are never meant to be permanent blessings.

I need you to know you are not at your Promised Land yet. I know stretching hurts, stretching leaves stretch marks and leaves us sore. I know "here" is comfortable and "there" is scary.

God had me write this book to say this: You are not at your Promised Land yet. Pack up your bags, gather up your belongings, and start moving forward.

As a child of God, our Spirit should never say, "I'm okay with good enough." Good enough will never be good enough when we were created for more than enough.

You will never reach your limits, so take off the limits you have placed on a limitless God. You were created to excel, to live an abundant life, to overcome obstacles, to beat addictions and so much more!

We have let good enough be good enough, long enough.

Stop settling and start stretching to the new things He has in store.

Stretch into your potential.

Stretch into your purpose.

Be grateful but that does not mean you have to settle.

Strive until you arrive.

Light My Fire

The same opportunity given to Terah was given to Abraham.

The Lord had said to Abram, "Go from your country, your people and your father's household to the land I will show you. I will make you into a great nation, and I will bless you; I will make your name great, and you will be a blessing. I will bless those who bless you, and whoever curses you I will curse; and all people on earth will be blessed through you." Abram went, as the Lord had told him… Abram was seventy-five years old when he set out from Harran. He took his wife Sarai, his nephew Lot, all the possessions they had accumulated and the people they had acquired in Harran, and they set out for the land of Canaan, and they arrived there. (Genesis 12:1-5) NIV

God told Abraham he would become a great nation, but his body was as good as dead. Abraham still had faith it was possible, so while waiting on God to start working, Abraham started walking. He walked all the way to Canaan. He did his part, even though God had not done His. In fact, Abraham had to wait twenty-five years for God to do His part.

Do you think he lost his fire? Of course he did. It took twenty-five years for God to fulfill His promise, but He eventually did. After Isaac was born, God goes crazy and asked Abraham to sacrifice his son Isaac on top of the mountain.

Early the next morning Abraham got up and loaded his donkey. He took with him two of his servants and his son Isaac. When he had cut enough wood for the burnt offering, he set out for the place God had told him about. On the third day Abraham looked up and saw the place in the distance. He said to his servants, "Stay here with the donkey while I and the boy go over there. We will worship and then we will come back to you." Abraham took the wood for the burnt offering and placed it on his son Isaac, and he himself carried the fire and the knife. (Genesis 22:3-6) NIV

Did you catch that? Abraham brought his own fire. Abraham knew there wasn't going to be a can of gasoline on top of that mountain so if he needed fire he was going to have to bring it himself. He wasn't waiting on God or depending on someone else to start his fire; he brought his own.

Too often we depend upon someone else to start our fire. Have you ever thought that maybe you were supposed to bring your own fire?

As God's child, the Holy Spirit lives within us. That means His fire is always available to us. It's time we stop waiting for someone else to give us confidence and start worshiping the One who can.

The next time discouragement comes knocking at your door, the next time conflict comes your way, tell yourself, "I have faith for this. I was built for this. If God is for me who can be against me? Greater is the One who is in me than the one who is coming against me."

The enemy can try to break me, but if he does, he's gonna find out what's inside of me. If he crushes me, he is going to find out I have Christ inside of me, which means I also have the presence and power of the Almighty God inside me. I'm pregnant with purpose!

I might be in the first trimester and things are getting a little nauseous, or I might be in the second trimester and things are getting a little uncomfortable, but I'm about to birth something.

I am not confident in myself but I am confident in the One who lives within me. Because He lives inside me, I am making up my mind today: I will be everything God has created me to be. I am not a seed of Abraham's father, I am a seed of Abraham.

So Abram went, as the Lord had told him….and they set out for the land of Canaan, and they arrived there. (Genesis 12:4) NIV

Let those words sink down into your soul: They arrived there.

They strived until they arrived.

He didn't rest until he stretched.

It's All About Jesus

As Paul concludes the passage on his inner conflict, he asks the most important question, "Who will rescue me from this body that is subject to death?"

He gives the most simple, yet most powerful answer, "Thanks be to God, who delivers me through Jesus Christ our Lord!" (Romans 7:25) NIV

Jesus is the answer to our conflict. Jesus is where our hope is found.

The only way you will ever be confident is to have a personal relationship with the One who created you.

Jesus became sin for YOU and died on the cross for YOU. He took the punishment of YOUR sin so YOU wouldn't have to. He defeated death so that anyone, and that includes you, who calls on the name of the Lord will be saved. All you have to do is accept Him as your Savior, trust in Him as Lord of your life, and you will be made right with God.

You can do that right now by praying these simple words:

Jesus, I trust in You. Jesus, I ask for forgiveness for my sin. Jesus, I invite You to be my Lord and Savior. I ask that Your power indwells me from this moment on. I ask that You give me the confidence to keep believing, no matter how conflicted I become. Thank You for dying on the cross to save me from my sins and arising again to give me a new life. Amen!

Congratulations. You have been placed "in Him," and His Spirit now lives within you.

With God we will gain the victory…Psalm 60:12 NIV

Including the victory over our inner enemy.

ACKNOWLEDGMENTS

Please allow me to take a minute and thank the people who helped make this book possible:

First of all, I would like to thank my wife, Amy. You have always been my inspiration and the most beautiful person I have ever met, inside and out. Because you are more than enough, I will never be able to get enough. My love for you is higher than the Olympus Mons and deeper than the Mariana Trench. I am amazed everyday by your class, character, and courage. Thank you for taking this journey with me…our best days are ahead. You are my Mickey, my Adrian, and my Apollo Creed. I wish I was more like you.

I would also like to thank my children, Noah and Eva. You didn't sign up for this, but here you are killing the game. I love you more than words can say. I am so proud of who you are and who you are becoming. I hope you are proud of me.

I would also like to thank my mom, dad, and two brothers. Where would I be without you? Seriously? You made me who I am today, and if that's not good enough, it's your fault. Just kidding. Kind of.

It is important I also thank the two churches that have allowed me to be their Pastor, Mountain View Church and West Tulsa FWB. The greatest privilege of my life was, and is, being your Pastor. I pray I have served you well.

A special thank you goes out to Kristina Duhaime and Andrea Gillispie for helping edit this book. You are grammatical geniuses and helped make a country boy sound more sophisticated than he really is.

Thank you Erinn Schaap for your awesome design skills and adding your magical touch to an otherwise boring word document.

Thank you Beatriz and Kerianne for making me look good.

Thank you Mountain View Staff. You are the "Dream Team."

Thank you Micahn Carter for preaching two of the best messages on Esau and Jesus I have ever heard. I give you the credit for those two chapters.

Thank you Bishop TD Jakes, Pastor Rick Warren, Pastor Andy Stanley, Pastor Craig Groeschel, Pastor Mark Batterson, Pastor Levi Lusko, and Pastor Mark Driscoll. I'm sure at some point I quoted you without giving proper credit as I have listened to each of you for several years. You have influenced my thinking beyond what I could ever repay.

Thank you Pastor Steven Furtick. Though we have never met, I feel like we are brothers from another mother. You have often been imitated, but never duplicated. How could you be? You are the best of my generation and I pray for you often.

Most importantly, I would like to thank my Lord and Savior, Jesus Christ. I am nothing without you. You owe me nothing because you have already given me everything.

Made in the USA
San Bernardino, CA
05 December 2018